Padre Pio *HIS LIFE AND MISSION*

MARY F. INGOLDSBY

Padre Pio
HIS LIFE AND MISSION

Veritas Publications Dublin

First published 1978 by
Veritas Publications,
7-8 Lower Abbey Street,
Dublin 1.

Reprinted 1984, 1986, 1988
Copyright © Mary F. Ingoldsby 1978

ISBN 0 905092 64 3

Nihil Obstat:
Richard Sherry, D.D.
Censor Deputatus

Imprimatur:
✠ Dermot,
Archbishop of Dublin.

The *nihil obstat* and *imprimatur* are a declaration that a text is
considered to be free of doctrinal or moral error. The do not necessarily
imply agreement with opinions expressed by the author.

Typography by Liam Miller
Cover design by Eddie McManus
Origination by Joe Healy Typesetting, Dublin.
Printed and bound in the Republic of Ireland
by Mount Salus Press Ltd., Dublin.

"I have been crucified with Christ:
it is no longer I who live
but Christ who lives in me"
(Gal 2:20).

Biographical Summary

1887   Born 25 May in Pietrelcina, southern Italy.

1903   Entered Capuchin novitiate.

1904-06 Secondary and philosophical studies.

1907   Solemn Profession.

1907-09 Theological studies.

1909-16 Spent mainly in his own home for health reasons.

1910   Ordained priest, 10 August, in Benevento Cathedral.

1915   Called up for military service, but sent home for a year's convalescence.

1916   Assigned to friary in San Giovanni Rotondo.

1917   Called up once more. Served in uniform for two months in Naples.

1922-31 Several interventions of Holy Office deprived him of many priestly faculties.

1933   Pope Pius XI restored him to complete freedom in priestly ministry.

1947   Building began on his hospital in San Giovanni Rotondo.

1956   Hospital officially opened on 5 May.

1959   New church inaugurated in San Giovanni Rotondo, 1 July.

1968   Prayer Groups formally approved by Holy See, 31 July.
Died at 2.30 a.m. on 23 September. Funeral rites 26 September. Crypt containing his tomb opened to public 27 September.

1969   Petition for opening of Cause for Beatification granted by Apostolic Administrator of Manfredonia.

1973   Archbishop of Manfredonia consigned to Holy See all documents required for formal introduction of Cause for Beatification and Canonisation of the Servant of God, Padre Pio of Pietrelcina, 16 January.

Contents

Preface

A well-known Italian Jesuit, Father Dominic Mondrone, who frequently visited San Giovanni Rotondo, has said that it will take an able biographer to depict Padre Pio as he really was, to paint a true pen-picture of him, free from the shadows which have blurred it up to the present.

I do not pretend to be that able biographer. All I have attempted is to give Padre Pio's devotees and other readers in the English-speaking world a more faithful picture of this extraordinary friar than was possible during his lifetime. The stigmatised priest of Mount Gargano wrote very little himself. However, during his early years as a Capuchin, separated for health reasons from his community, he corresponded constantly with his spiritual directors. It was only after his death in 1968 that these letters became public property. Three volumes of his correspondence have been published in Italian since 1970. The first and by far the most important contains his letters to his spiritual directors (1910-1922).[1] It has been my privilege to translate this volume into English, an inspiring and enriching experience which kept me in San Giovanni Rotondo for nearly two years, close to the tomb of the servant of God. Week by week, month by month these letters trace the spiritual ascent of this twentieth-century mystic and reveal his exceptional gifts and charisms which were to make him what he eventually became: a crucified priest, a victim for souls, a most intimate collaborator in Christ's redemptive mission. While translation of his letters provided me with much valuable material for the present work, I also had an opportunity in San Giovanni Rotondo to read much literature published in Italian since his death. An amount of valuable information emerged from perusal of *Voce di Padre Pio,* the official organ of the cause for his beatification, issued monthly since 1970 by his Capuchin friary. Among other things its pages contain the testimony of many visiting prelates and the witness of a number of friars who lived with Padre Pio in that remote but now quite famous friary.[2]

A great deal has already been written in English, well and less well, on the subject of this disconcerting Capuchin friar. Fantastic tales have not been lacking and some irresponsible or insufficiently informed writers have misrepresented the facts. Hence a lot of inexact information has been circulated with regard to Padre Pio of Pietrelcina. Although the present work lays no claim to special merit, the writer does claim to have rigorously excluded all that could not be sifted at the sources in the friary where he spent most of his life and in his home town of Pietrelcina from which he wrote a great many of his letters.

Resident in Italy since 1939, I had heard quite a lot about Padre Pio. From 1946 to 1958, as the delegate of a worldwide Catholic organisation, I was constantly on the move from the Alps to Sicily and frequently came on groups of his enthusiastic admirers. I cannot say I was impressed, as many of those who spoke so vehemently in favour of the stigmatist of Mount Gargano struck me as more than a little fanatical. In those postwar years when Italy's social fabric was still badly torn and her Church life disorganised, there were alleged "apparitions" and "revelations" in many parts of the country. Our Blessed Lady was said to have appeared in several different regions and crowds were rushing to these places in a kind of frenzied hunt for solace and consolation. It was in this context that I first heard of Padre Pio and, in my ignorance of the true facts, I labelled him as just one more case of that postwar religious psychosis. I had no intention of setting out for the little town where he was to be found. It was only in 1956 that a series of quite unforeseen circumstances brought me in the depths of winter to San Giovanni Rotondo, where I assisted at his extraordinary Mass and came face to face with him personally. In the course of that brief visit my ideas underwent a total change. I bought some reliable books about him, notably a volume (no longer in print) containing the doctors' reports on his extraordinary medical history. From that time onward, discounting the fanaticism which continued to surround him, I no longer had any doubts as to the extraordinary nature of his life and mission.

No pen will ever be adequate to paint the portrait of a

great mystic, who is, in the last analysis, a masterpiece of God's creative hand. All one can do is to approach the task with deepest reverence, doing one's utmost not to spoil or obscure the image.

I acknowledge with deep gratitude the kind help given to me by the Capuchin community in San Giovanni Rotondo, who allowed me to make use of their publications which are amply quoted in the present work. I am greatly indebted to Padre Gerardo Di Flumeri, Delegate Postulator of Padre Pio's Cause and general editor of Padre Pio of Pietrelcina Editions; and also in a particular way to Father Joseph Pius, the American member of the community who was privileged to assist Padre Pio during the last three years of his life and who shed much light for me on many aspects of that holy life. I am grateful, moreover, to all those who have kindly allowed me to use their Italian texts and to many others on whose oral reports I have freely drawn.

MARY F. INGOLDSBY

Prologue

Most Catholics nowadays have heard of Padre Pio, the humble Capuchin friar who spent the greater part of his long life in a rugged village high up on Mount Gargano. To those less familiar with Italy, the Gargano Peninsula is best identified geographically as the "spur" on the Italian "boot", a barren headland jutting out into the Adriatic and forming the extreme northern belt of the otherwise fertile Apulian region.

Padre Pio was thirty-one when he received the bleeding imprint of the wounds of Christ's passion. That was in 1918, when World War I had left Europe scarred and bewildered, when ruin and desolation were the lot of most families in the Mediterranean area who were trying to pick up the threads of normal living. In the midst of this desolate scene a message went out from Mount Gargano, a news item was rapidly circulated concerning this extraordinary friar who fixed men's eyes on a totally different reality, a man whose presence spoke of God more eloquently than the best of sermons. His call was a call to the supernatural in the midst of postwar chaos, a call to fervent Christian life, to reform of morals, to peace and brotherly love, to a life in which prayer would prevail over material interests. His call, moreover, was substantiated by indisputable signs of his close union with God, with Christ crucified, with the Virgin Mother of God in whom he invited all men to place their filial trust.

Padre Pio read men's hearts, he obtained extraordinary temporal and spiritual favours, he possessed the quite exceptional charisms of bilocation, prophecy, the gift of tongues, the power of healing, while hundreds if not thousands can testify to the extraordinary fragrance which emanated from his bleeding wounds and from his whole person. These phenomena exerted an irresistible attraction upon thousands of people who had had their fill of war and horror and seen the collapse of earthly ideals. They hastened in growing numbers to that remote mountain village, San Giovanni Rotondo, from which nobody seemed to come away without experiencing a radical change of life.

Who was Padre Pio and what was his secret? To all outward appearances he was a poor Italian friar like any of his brethren, with a family history similar to theirs. But in reality he was utterly different, an exceptional soul in every way from the time of his birth.

From his own lips, when he was halfway through his mortal life, we gather a precious testimony to this effect. "From the time of my birth God favoured me in a most special manner. He showed me that he would not only be my Saviour and supreme benefactor, but my devoted, sincere and faithful friend, the friend of my heart, my infinite love and consolation, my joy and comfort, my entire wealth."[1] Once, in later life, a woman whom he directed in the spiritual life noticed an expression of great suffering on his face and was forced to exclaim: "Father, you are in pain! You have suffered a great deal all through your life!" "Even in my mother's womb!" was Padre Pio's surprising reply, from which we understand that even before birth he was conscious of suffering.[2]

How could this be possible? A great master of the spiritual life, St Francis de Sales, in his famous *Treatise on the Love of God,* enlightens us. He tells us that some souls, only a very few, are privileged to receive exceptional gifts of grace and light and love *even in their mother's womb,* because they are destined to fulfil some great human and divine mission. Is it too much to believe that Padre Pio of Pietrelcina, the first stigmatised priest in the history of the Church, was one of that chosen few? The facts, supported by ample documentary evidence, would seem to justify this belief. The millions of lives over which he exerted and still exerts a powerful influence for good seem to point unmistakably in this direction.[3]

ONE

Early Years

Francesco Forgione, the future Padre Pio, came into the world like any ordinary mortal, without any special signs to prefigure his greatness.

It was 9 a.m. on 26 May 1887 when his father, Grazio, a hardworking small farmer, climbed the steps of the village hall in Pietrelcina to see the mayor who kept the register of births. At 5 p.m. the previous day his wife, Maria Giuseppa De Nunzio, aged 28, had given birth to a boy, who was baptised in the church of St Mary of the Angels and named Francesco. Only the witnesses, a bootmaker named Pennisi and a farmer called Orlando, signed the register, for Grazio, the father of the newborn baby who was to be known to the world as Padre Pio, was illiterate and unable even to sign his name. That was not the first occasion on which he had shamefacedly admitted his inability to write. He had already done so when registering the birth of Michele, Padre Pio's elder brother. He was to do so again when five more children were born. A boy and a girl died in infancy. Another girl, Felicità, died in her late twenties. Pellegrina died at 52 while Grazia, the youngest, became Sister Pius of the Sorrowful Mother in the Bridgettine Convent in Rome and died less than a year after Padre Pio.

According to his mother, Francesco was "a quiet and tranquil baby". She also tells us that he was never troublesome as a little boy, that he always obeyed his parents and went morning and evening to the church to pay a visit to Jesus and Mary. During the day he didn't go out to join in the noisy games of his companions. Sometimes his mother would urge him to go out to play with the others, but he used to refuse and say: "I don't want to play with them because they use bad language."

A visit to Padre Pio's birthplace, easily accessible now that the autostrada links Naples with Bari and passes close to

Benevento, is well worth while. Pietrelcina is about six miles from Benevento. June is an ideal month in which to enjoy the beauty of the landscape on which Padre Pio's eyes so often rested and which he carried in his heart throughout his long life. As you drive along the pleasant road from Benevento the little town comes suddenly into view, much the same as when Padre Pio glimpsed it each time he returned home. The only difference is the imposing Capuchin friary which now dominates the scene, built in the thirties and taken over by the Capuchins in 1947 after invading armies had occupied it during World War II.

Pietrelcina is one of those little, out of the way rural spots which God seems to choose for preference when he intends to communicate some important message to men. Lourdes and Fatima were little-known hamlets until the Immaculate Mother of God chose to make them famous. The recipients of both those messages which were to have a lasting effect on the world were poor little rural children. The exceptional message which Padre Pio was to communicate to all parts of the world and which is still going out to the ends of the earth from his simple tomb in San Giovanni Rotondo— essentially a call to genuine Christian life, a challenge to our comfortable consumer brand of Christianity – had its origins in Pietrelcina, just such another remote rural centre as Fatima or Lourdes.

Francesco Forgione, the future stigmatised priest, first saw the light in Rione Castello, the castle district of the town, which takes its name from the baronial castle around which the original group of small dwellings rose up in medieval days. Time appears to have stood still there since those days. The tiny houses hug one another closely, the streets are narrow and cannot be entered by car, for at intervals the steep ascent calls for steps cut in the rock instead of a roadway. The visitor has to climb steeply by the paths and alleys Padre Pio knew so well. His old home at 27 Vico Storto Valla has been acquired by the local Capuchins and is preserved in its primitive state: rough stone floors, unadorned walls, the open fireplace at which his energetic mother, Mamma Peppa (short for Giuseppa, Josephine), cooked the family meals, the humble bedroom in which Francesco was born and the *torretta,* or tower, on the opposite side of the narrow street, to which Padre Pio used to retire to pray and study when he lived in his own home, first as a Capuchin student and later as a young priest.

We can easily reconstruct the domestic environment into which he was born. The humble furnishings of the home are still there, with the kitchen utensils and simple equipment which served the family's needs. All this shows a poverty and simplicity which startle the visitor accustomed to the items which appear so necessary in a modern home. However, although poor in this world's goods the Forgione family never lacked what was necessary and the future Padre Pio never went hungry or barefoot. His parents were industrious and hardworking and Mamma Peppa in particular was greatly respected by the townsfolk. Straight and slim, she had, in the opinion of her neighbours, the manners and bearing of a lady, an innate nobility often to be found in southern Italian rural folk.

Pietrelcina today is not very different from the little town in which Padre Pio grew up. The people still live mainly on the proceeds of their own hard work in the fields. Most families have an acre or two of land just outside the town which provides them with the main items of their diet. Although this is not a wine-producing region, almost every family has a small vineyard of its own. The principal crops marketed today are grain and tobacco. Perhaps the only difference nowadays at harvest time is the presence of a few tractors and some other farm machinery. The rest must surely be just as it was in Padre Pio's youth. The little homes are pleasantly cool on a summer's day. From the tiny windows of Padre Pio's own home the view is breath-taking: a wide rolling valley with well cultivated fields, stretching away to the mountains of this Samnium region, an offshoot of the Apennine Chain which is Italy's backbone. As you drive through the surrounding country, gospel scenes and parables are brought vividly to mind: the labourers in the vineyard, the new wine which cannot be put into old wineskins, the barren fig tree, the plentiful harvest awaiting the workers.

Our Lord's parables and images were drawn from the scenes and situations familiar to his Palestinian listeners and, in point of fact, southern Italy is quite similar to the land in which Christ was born and the life style and habits of the two rural populations differ very little.

In later life Padre Pio sometimes allowed his friends to glimpse his nostalgia for his humble home and the simple folk with whom he spent his boyhood. He was perfectly frank in referring to the poverty of his own home and often said: "In my home it was hard to find a ten lire piece, but we never lacked anything necessary." He also recalled the "divine gifts" received in that simple rural atmosphere where everything was so genuine, honest and wholesome. "Perhaps the dear simple people of those days will be seen no more", he sometimes remarked with a hint of sadness. He himself was a typical product of that environment. When he had fully matured in age and grace he showed forth the fine qualities inbred in the people of his region: a keen sense of humour and the sound commonsense of the Pietrelcina folk. When he wanted to get rid of a crowd of admirers and devotees, he did it as if he were driving a flock of sheep, with the gestures of the former shepherd boy.

As a small boy Francesco was inclined to withdraw from the company of those of his own age, but this did not mean that he was sullen or surly. He was an ingenuous boy, somewhat silent and reserved, but with no trace of arrogance.

Mary Pyle[1], who lived for more than 40 years in San Giovanni Rotondo as a spiritual daughter of Padre Pio, knew his parents well. It was in the house she built close to the Capuchin friary that both of his parents spent their last years and passed peacefully away, assisted by their stigmatised son. This American lady had visited many countries including Portugal. Her comment on Padre Pio's parents was that Grazio and Giuseppa reminded her remarkably of the parents of Giacinta and Francesco Marto, the little seers of Fatima, even in appearance, but especially by reason of their graciousness, hospitality, uprightness and that real dignity which is typical of simple country folk. They too were affectionately known as *Zi,* like the Fatima parents. The Italian *Zi,* an abbreviation of *Zio,* uncle, denotes a close bond of affection even when a man is not a relative. Mr Marto was and will always be *Zi Marto.* Padre Pio's father had been baptised Orazio (Horace), but an erroneous entry in the birth register made him Grazio, a masculine version of the name Grace. He was so convinced that his name was Grazio that he even celebrated as his name-day the feast of Our Lady of Grace. Both parents were slim and wiry, with workworn hands. In their tiny home a serene and cheerful spirit reigned and Mamma Peppa cared for her children diligently, with true motherly love. Thus, as a boy, Francesco lacked nothing that makes for a child's happiness, the warmth of his parents' love, good simple food and adequate clothing.

Francesco was already favoured with exceptional graces at that early age, although nothing of this was apparent externally or even suspected by those around him. Padre Agostino of San Marco in Lamis, his confessor during student days and while he was a young priest, assures us that Padre Pio's ecstasies and apparitions began when he was only five years of age, and that already at that early age he had made up his mind to give himself entirely to God. From that time onward he was favoured continually with visions. When Padre Agostino asked him in 1915 how it was that he had never revealed these things, he replied candidly that he had said nothing because he thought they happened to everyone. At five years of age he was also the object of the devil's attacks which recurred frequently for almost twenty years. The devil often appeared to him in obscene forms, as a human or a beast. Padre Pio told his confessor that he had been troubled by the appearance of hideous creatures even in early infancy.

His vocation and the action of God's grace in him at a very early age explain his tendency to withdraw from his companions. The attraction he felt for prayer was soon evident. Padre Raffaele of Sant'Elia passes on to us what another friar of Padre Pio's own age told him, a friar who had lived quite close to the Forgione family in Pietrelcina:

My own mother told me that when Padre Pio was nine or ten years old he had a particular love for pious books, in which he would bury himself instead of going out to play. Moreover, when Mass was ended and the sacristan closed the church, young Francesco used to ask to be left there alone. He would beg the sacristan not to let anyone know and would arrange the hour at which the man was to let him out. Already at that age his conduct revealed his deep interior life: he was always docile to his parents and respectful to all those around him. Already, too, the value of suffering and expiation were present to his young mind. He accepted cheerfully any suffering that came his way and in addition imposed penances on himself which caused him real suffering. His mother found him one day scourging himself with a chain and tried to stop him, but the boy told her he was "doing it for Jesus who had been scourged by the soldiers until his blood flowed".[2]

Padre Pio seldom referred to the extraordinary divine gifts with which he was favoured, but occasionally he let slip a word or two, after which he would close up at once as if he regretted having spoken. From an odd word or phrase which escaped him when surrounded by his friends and intimates, added to the witness of those who grew up along with him, we get quite a distinct picture of the early life of this genuine mystic. Although incomplete and sometimes coloured a little too highly by those who relate the facts, the substance remains and the truth emerges.

His father emigrated twice, first to South America when Francesco was quite young, and later to the United States. Padre Pio himself ruefully told the story of his father's disillusionment the first time he crossed the ocean. A man from Pietrelcina had gone to South America and had written home about the riches he had acquired, saying, among other things, that "the houses were roofed with golden tiles". Padre Pio used to make fun in later years of his ingenuous fellow-townsmen who, on hearing the emigrant's story, decided to go out in a group to this wonderful country where riches could be amassed so quickly. Some of them sold all they had in order to pay the fare, but on arrival they found their boastful fellow-townsman washing dishes in a restaurant. He was so crestfallen when he saw them that they hadn't the heart to reproach him. They moved from place to place without finding work and before long returned home, where some had debts to pay. Poorer than when he left home, Grazio Forgione continued, however, to pay for his son's studies. Some years later he emigrated to the United States.

Luigi Orlando, who grew up with Francesco Forgione, sheds light on his life as a teenager. Francesco's family entrusted him with two sheep which he used to take to graze at Piana Romana, while his companion Luigi had one sheep to look after. While the sheep grazed the boys would tumble about and wrestle. Francesco nearly always got the better of his opponent because he was a couple of years older and was bigger. "One day," says Luigi, "when he had pinned me down and continued to hold me, in the effort to throw him off I let slip a bad word, at which Francesco immediately jumped up and ran away. He couldn't bear bad language and never used even the slightest improper word himself." The same companion tells how Francesco used to build with great care and devotion a little Christmas crib in a niche in his home, with the *Bambinello,* Our Lady and St Joseph, illuminated by tiny oil-lamps which he made by filling shells with oil and floating a wick in them. According to Orlando and others, he was just an ordinary boy, but quieter and rather better-mannered than the rest, a youngster of few words who never spoke about himself.

When he was ten years old Francesco had a mysterious illness and was in bed for over a month on a very strict diet. The local doctor tried every remedy he knew but the boy remained very ill. His mother was in great distress as she had to look after the patient and at the same time attend to the farm, for the harvesting was at its peak. One day the doctor told her not to leave the sick boy alone, fearing he might die from one hour to the next. He left some tablets near him, which the patient didn't touch. His mother felt sure that only Our Lady of the Libera could save him.[3] She was obliged to set out that day as usual for the farm at Piana Romana, but she first prepared an abundant dish of fried peppers, some of which she took with her for the harvesters.

Many years later Padre Pio told his friends how he could smell the appetising odour of those peppers in the next room but hadn't the courage to ask for some. But no sooner was his mother gone than Francesco got up, went to the kitchen and devoured a large quantity of the savoury peppers. Feeling very satisfied he went back to bed and fell fast asleep. His face was soon as red as the peppers he had eaten. When his mother returned, alarmed at his appearance she sent at once for the doctor, who found the boy's pulse and heartbeat quite normal and was unable to explain the sudden improvement. Next morning Francesco felt fine and again taking advantage of his mother's absence he dressed and set off for Piana Romana, which was half-an-hour's walk from his home.[4] He was completely restored to health by the pure air out on the farm, beneath the famous elm tree where he was to experience such extraordinary things a few years later. The elm is now plasticised and enclosed in the room behind the altar of the chapel on the spot where Padre Pio first received the stigmata in 1910.

Padre Pio sometimes told his intimates the story of the cigar. One day Padre Raffaele asked him if he had ever smoked, to which he replied that he had — once! "I was probably ten years old", he said, "when *Zi Pellegrino* called me one day and said: 'Francesco, you're quick on your feet. Here's some money, go and buy me a *toscano* (a cheap cigar smoked by country folk in Italy) and a box of matches.'" Francesco was off at once, but on his way back it occurred to him to stop for a moment to find out what it was like to smoke. He struck a match and lit the cigar, and as he took the first whiff his stomach turned and he actually fell. It seemed to him as if the world had turned upside down. After a few minutes the nausea passed and he went back to the farm and told his uncle Pellegrino what he had done. His uncle laughed heartily, but little Francesco's head was still spinning and from that day he had a real aversion to smoking.[5]

Although Francesco was already ten he had not been sent to school. His elder brother had gone several years earlier but had learned very little, so his father was disinclined to send the younger boy at all. Then one day he asked Francesco if he wanted to go to school, to which he replied that he certainly did. "Well, if you learn something there and don't do as your brother did," said his father, "your dad will make you a monk." But Francesco continued to tend his father's sheep and his schooling remained in the realm of promises. Finally, after several promises unfulfilled, the boy asked, "Dad, when are you going to send me to school?" That evening Grazio spoke to his wife and they decided to send Francesco to study privately, as he was far past the age for beginners. At last he left the sheep and took up his books. The teacher chosen was a certain Domenico Tizzani, an ex-priest. For three years Francesco attended this private school, where he completed his primary education. But immediately after this he showed a real disinclination to study. Some people report that Padre Pio told them how the sight of that schoolmaster filled him with fear, as if he were the devil himself, but his official biographers doubt this very much. Others attribute his reluctance to continue his studies to the recurrence of illness. A lot of fantastic tales have been told about the behaviour of this ex-priest and the family he created after leaving the priesthood, but Padre Pio always spoke kindly of him and said he was "a good teacher" and that he was "reserved and never referred to his private life in the presence of his pupils". Their relationship was a fortunate one for the ex-priest, as Padre Pio recounted more than once. Shortly after his own ordination Padre Pio, passing close to the house of his former teacher, saw the daughter on the doorstep evidently in great distress. He asked how the teacher was, at which the girl burst into tears and told him he was very ill. Padre Pio asked to see him and was admitted to the bedroom. Both men were deeply moved. No other priest had had the courage to visit the sick man, but through Padre Pio he made his peace with God and died only a few days later. Whenever he told this story, Padre Pio was always very touched and would raise his eyes to heaven to implore the divine mercy for sinners.

Apart from attending school, Francesco went to Mass each morning during this period and to Benediction in the afternoon. Grazio tells us: "One day my wife went to see the schoolteacher to find out how he was getting on, only to be told: 'He's not making any headway, and no wonder, since he's always in church. The morning at Mass, the evening again

in church, so how can he learn anything?'" The poor woman
returned home quite upset and as soon as Francesco came
from church she started to reprimand him. Francesco listened
in silence, but as his mother continued to scold him and went
so far as to say: "What am I going to write to your father
who emigrated to America in order to pay for your studies
and make you a monk?" the boy was almost in tears and
replied: "Mother, it isn't my going to church that prevents
me from learning. It's just that that man is a bad priest!"
At this the mother was silent. Grazio continues: "While this
was happening in Italy, I was saying to myself in America:
'This son of mine must become a monk, but what can he
learn from an unfrocked priest?' So I wrote to my wife telling her to take him away from that man and send him to a
better teacher."[6]

Mamma Giuseppa brought her young son at once to a
teacher named Angelo Caccavo, who ran a private school at
the time and taught later as a state teacher for thirty years.
At first he did not want to accept the new pupil, for fear of
offending his former teacher, but when the mother and some
of her relatives insisted, he gave in. As Giuseppa went down
the steps after handing him over to the teacher, she turned
back and said: "Teacher, I have to work on the farm, so I
am leaving him in your hands. *Beat* him if necessary." Francesco heard these words but said nothing, because he adored
his mother and accepted whatever she said. He joined the
class and was soon in the first place. This teacher became
very fond of him in view of his docility and diligent application to his books. But Francesco got a beating on one occasion when some of his classmates had played a trick on him.
One of the girls wrote a love letter and found an opportunity
to slip it into Francesco's pocket. The pupils began coughing
to attract the teacher's attention, and when asked what was
wrong they told him that Francesco had been flirting with
the girl in question. Interrogated by the master, Francesco
continued to deny it. Then he was searched and the declaration of love was found in his pocket. "Aha!" said the master,
"so you are the one that is going to be a monk! And you have
told lies too." Then he started to beat him soundly. Next

day the little girl was very remorseful and owned up to the trick they had played on Francesco. Many years later Padre Pio told this story quite candidly to his friends and added: "Poor Mr Caccavo, he was very upset about it, but as regards the beating, nobody took it back!"[7]

Apart from this little incident Francesco never had the slightest trouble with his new teacher. He was very bright and in two years completed the three-year lower secondary-school course. He was then fourteen years old and he wrote to his father in America to tell him how well he was getting on. In the records in San Giovanni Rotondo there are some copybooks containing essays he wrote at this stage of his education, which show clearly the fruit he derived from his schooling, his firm Christian principles and his solid piety.

As a student in the Capuchin scholasticate later, he wrote affectionate letters to his former teacher, who remained very fond of him, although without sharing his religious views. When he was already established in San Giovanni Rotondo, after which he never returned to his native Pietrelcina, Padre Pio wrote to Mr Caccavo on 11 May 1919:

I myself am very well, but am kept busy day and night with hundreds and even thousands of confessions. I always remember you in my poor prayers before the Lord, and God alone knows how I insist with him for your total conversion. I should be very happy if I could see you again and embrace you here, because it is impossible for me to return to my home town. I send greetings to all and a warm embrace, praying that God's grace may keep and sustain you.[8]

TWO

Vocation

We have it on good authority that Francesco Forgione thought of consecrating his life to God when he was only five years old. From that time onwards his resolution grew stronger, which is borne out by some unusual facts related about his early boyhood. As we know, his schooling began later than that of most children, at ten years of age, when his father finally decided to take him from work on the farm and give him a chance to prove his worth at his books. He received private tuition from more than one tutor and at one stage was taken in hand for lessons in mathematics by a young priest named Don Nicola Caruso. To this priest Francesco confided that on more than one occasion when he returned from school he found on the threshold of his home a stranger dressed as a priest, who tried to prevent him passing. Each time this happened, Francesco stopped there on the spot. Then a small barefooted boy would arrive and make the sign of the cross, after which the stranger immediately vanished and the boy was free to enter his home. This testimony may be added to a number of others which assert that the future Padre Pio began to be troubled by diabolical temptations at a very early age. We learn from his own writings that these temptations continued for several decades.

His mother herself and several companions of his own age have left us accounts of the penances which the future Capuchin inflicted on his frail body even in early boyhood. A priest named Giuseppe Orlando, who also coached Francesco privately for a while, tells us that he reprimanded him for "disobeying his mother who had prepared a comfortable bed for him, while he preferred to sleep on the floor with a stone for his pillow". A young fellow named Ubaldo Vecchiarino used to go on the long winter evenings with some merry companions to spy on Francesco, to find out what kept him shut up at home instead of joining their

lighthearted company. They used to place one stone on top
of another until they could reach the little window of his
room and peep in. The room was in darkness, but they often
heard the sound of someone scourging his body with a rope.[1]

At the age of fifteen Francesco was ready to carry out his
holy purpose of embracing the religious life and it only
remained to decide where he was to go. His mother had
entrusted him to the care of the local parish priest, Don
Salvatore Pannullo, a zealous and cultured man, who at a
later stage witnessed several extraordinary events in the
young Capuchin's life. Now in his early teens, Francesco
became an altar-boy with others of his own age. He frequented
the sacraments regularly, attended all the religious services
and devotions and kept away from his more worldly-minded
companions. He lived more or less apart and his life was
divided between his studies and the church. He spoke many
times to his mother, to the parish priest and also to his uncle
Pellegrino of his strong desire to enter religious life. His
father was in North America at this time.

Pietrelcina is not far from Morcone, where there was a
Capuchin friary and novitiate. Brother Camillo of Sant'Elia,
a fervent friar with a flowing dark beard, was a familiar
figure in Padre Pio's home town to which he came at regular
intervals to collect alms. He always had a kind word and a
caress for the children and sometimes gave them a chestnut,
a walnut, or else a medal or holy picture. Little Francesco
was greatly attracted to this simple and humble son of St
Francis and found it hard to tear himself away from him.
However, he kept this a secret in his earlier years. Now, in
his fifteenth year, his family began to discuss his desire to
give himself to God and the first approaches were made.
His uncle spoke to the parish priest who in turn wrote to
the Capuchin Provincial in Foggia. But the latter replied
that the boy must wait as their novitiate was full. Meanwhile
his uncle began to tell Francesco that he would have to wait
many months before he could enter the Capuchins and
suggested he go instead to the Benedictines of Montevergine.
"Those monks dress well," he said, "they wear hats and shoes
and are quite comfortably off." Francesco already knew the

shrine of Our Lady on Montevergine, where he had gone on pilgrimage more than once with his uncle and cousins, but he replied decidedly: "No, I don't want to go there because they haven't got beards." His uncle also suggested the Redemptorists, "who dress as priests and live comfortably", and then the Franciscans, "quite plump and well fed, not like those friars in Morcone who all look consumptive". But Francesco was not to be moved from his purpose. "I want to join the friars who have beards", he insisted and nothing could dissuade him from this idea. In later years Padre Pio often told his friends quite candidly, "Fra Camillo's beard was vividly before me all the time and nothing could make me change my mind."

However, after a couple of months a reply came from the Provincial of the Capuchins to say that Francesco could come, so it was now up to the parish priest, Don Salvatore, to prepare the necessary papers for his admission to the novitiate.

At this stage a new and altogether surprising element entered into the situation. It was rumoured that Francesco was flirting with the station-master's daughter! Don Salvatore came down to earth with a jolt. To think that he had considered young Forgione the most exemplary of all his altar boys! Astonished but not completely convinced by the unpleasant discovery which had been revealed in an anonymous letter, he called an urgent meeting of the other priests of the parish. (We have this story from Padre Raffaele of Sant'Elia, who got it from Padre Pio himself.) The priests discussed the matter, then called Francesco and, without mentioning the anonymous letter, they informed him that he was excluded henceforth from serving during the religious ceremonies. Meanwhile they kept a strict watch on his movements to see if he were meeting the girl in question. To make matters worse in their opinion, the girl hardly ever came to church. In reality, Francesco didn't even know her.

Seeing the parish priest's changed attitude towards him, the young aspirant to Capuchin life wondered what had happened. He searched his conscience for an answer but could find none. In the end he concluded that this must be something they did to a boy who intended to become a friar, a test to see the sort of stuff of which the candidate was made. A month or so passed in this way and the day for his departure loomed. The priests were to prepare his papers, but how could they do this for a candidate who behaved in such a way? Investigations continued, but there was no evidence of any misdemeanour on Francesco's part. Then the priest responsible for the enquiries identified the writer of the anonymous letter, who confessed all. The culprit was another altar-boy who had been moved by pure jealousy. He wanted to show Francesco up in a bad light in the eyes of the parish priest who had always tended to single him out for special favour.

Once the truth was out, the parish priest tried to make reparation for such unjust treatment. He called the other priests together and summoned Francesco who found himself as if before a court which was to try him for some crime. He trembled and wondered what would happen next. But Don Salvatore said kindly: "My boy, we were punishing you for something you didn't do, but since we have discovered your innocence you must take up your duties in church as before, and as a reward for your docility under this trial we intend to provide you with your papers for the novitiate free of charge, so that you may go without delay to the Capuchins in Morcone." Francesco heaved a deep sigh of relief, thanked them, then remained for a long while in church to pray and to thank Our Lady Liberatrix.

Here we have a second instance of calumny, which was not to be the last in the life of the stigmatised friar. He never bore malice towards the writer of that anonymous letter or towards the schoolgirl who had written the love-letter alleged to have come from his hand. He was to tell his spiritual director later that it never crossed his mind to have a vengeful spirit towards those who calumniated him. "I prayed for them," he said, "and I continue to pray. I sometimes said to the Lord that if it were necessary to treat them harshly in order to convert them, he should do so, as long as he saved them in the end."[2]

All was now in order for Francesco's departure from home to embrace the austere life of the Capuchin novitiate for which he yearned. He was to leave immediately after the

Christmas holidays. His father was still absent in America and his mother was not a good traveller, so it was decided that two of his former tutors, Mr Caccavo and Don Nicola Caruso, should accompany him to Morcone, a distance of only about twenty-five miles but quite a journey in those days of primitive transport and rough roads. On the night before his departure from his father's house Francesco was consoled by a remarkable vision. He was always very reluctant to set down in writing any of his extraordinary mystical experiences and it was only when obliged by obedience that he gave an account of this vision in some autobiographical notes which appear as an appendix to the first volume of his *Letters*. In these notes, as in many passages of his letters in which he describes the most sublime phenomena of his mystical life, Padre Pio, like many another mystic, writes in the third person and refers to himself as "that soul". He gives a graphic description of this vision. He beheld "a majestic figure of rare beauty, radiant as the sun", who showed him a great multitude divided into two groups, "men of beautiful countenance clad in snow-white garments" and "hideous blackrobed figures". In the midst of the two groups "a man advanced, so tall that his forehead touched the clouds, and with the face of a hideous black monster". His guide informed him that he would have to fight this monster, that he must fight courageously and not lose heart, for he would be assisted by this same heavenly guide. He entered into combat with the monster and after a dreadful struggle succeeded in putting him to flight. All the hideous creatures then fled with deafening cries and imprecations, while the whiterobed throng applauded. This vision, he said, "filled him with such great courage that it seemed like a thousand years before he was able to abandon the world for ever". By a further vision, purely intellectual this time, "the Lord was pleased to manifest the meaning of the symbolical vision" and he understood in a flash that "his entry into religion meant exposure to combat with that mysterious being with whom he had fought in the first vision". He knew then that although the demons would be present at his battles to make fun of his failures, there was nothing to fear, "because the angels would be present to applaud his victories over Satan". "This vision", he continues, "made that soul strong and generous in bidding farewell to the world."[3]

On the morning of 6 January 1903, then, we find the future Padre Pio saying goodbye to his mother, brother, sisters and other relatives. He kissed the parish priest's hand and went on his knees to receive his mother's blessing. "My son," said Mamma Peppa, "my heart is breaking, but St Francis is calling you and you must go." Not many days later, on 22 January, after the customary retreat, Francesco knelt at the high altar of the friary church in Morcone and was clothed in the habit of a Capuchin novice, receiving the name Fra Pio of Pietrelcina, a name that was to resound far and wide in the years that followed and continues to reverberate throughout the Catholic world today.

We can imagine the happiness that flooded the boy's soul at this first decisive break with the world and family ties, the peace and joy he experienced in finding himself at last in the clothing of a follower of St Francis, the garb of poverty and love for which he had so ardently longed. All the fervour of a novice was his. He delighted in his newfound "freedom" which to the world would appear imprisonment, freedom to devote himself heart and soul to his Lord and Saviour in the observance of a strict rule of prayer, fasting and penance. First fervour in religious life, experienced during novitiate days, can dwindle and die or at least grow cold, as it does in the case of religious who make no progress on the path mapped out for them by God. In the case of Francesco Forgione, novitiate fervour was to increase as the years passed, and love for his crucified Saviour was to be heated white-hot, to the point at which he could think of nothing but the sufferings of his Lord and Master and felt impelled to offer himself as a victim, an offering which he repeated over and over again as the years went by. His thirst for suffering was never quenched. The more he suffered the more he yearned to suffer. God heard his plea and drew him along the path of extraordinary suffering, allowing him to share in the very passion of Christ, which came to be mysteriously re-enacted in this ecstatic stigmatised friar of Mount Gargano.

His letters to his spiritual directors return constantly to this theme.

I am happier than ever when I am suffering and if I were to listen to the promptings of my heart, I should ask Jesus to give me all the sufferings of men. But I do not do this because I am afraid of being too selfish by desiring the better part, which is suffering (2-4-1912). I love the Cross, the Cross alone. I love it because I see it always on Jesus' shoulders. Jesus is well aware that my entire life, my whole heart is consecrated to him and to his sufferings (1-2-1913). I long for death for no other reason than to be united by indissoluble bonds with the heavenly Bridegroom. Yet I desire to live in order to suffer more and more, for Jesus has given me to understand that the sure proof of love is only to be found in suffering (6-5-1913).

All the great spiritual writers tell us that the road to higher states of prayer and spiritual experience is opened up by mortification and austerity of life. Intimacy with God, with the maker of heaven and earth, cannot be bought except at the price of mortification of the flesh and the senses. Such ideas are foreign to the minds of those who give themselves up to the pleasures of this world. They are foreign even to a great many Christians today. All the baptised are called to holiness and union with God, but the majority remain spiritually stunted, like plants deprived of light and air.

* * * * *

Those who assisted at the simple ceremony of clothing of a group of Capuchin novices on that January morning over seventy years ago could have had no inkling of the immense mission in store for one of them. The bald account of the ceremony as it appears in the Register of Clothings in Morcone gives us no clue. It runs as follows:

Morcone, 22 January 1903. Fra Pio of Pietra Elcina, known in the world as Francesco Forgione, son of Grazio and Maria Giuseppa Di Nunzio, born in Pietra Elcina in the province and archdiocese of Benevento on 25 May 1887, baptised, confirmed in the parish of Our Lady of the Angels on 27 September 1899, in accordance with

the order received from the Very Reverend Commissary General
of the Province of Sant'Angelo was temporarily clothed in the
habit by me, Fra Tommaso of Monte Sant'Angelo, Master of Novices,
on 22 January 1903 at 9 o'clock in the morning, in our church of
Morcone before the main altar, in the presence of the professed
religious and the novices.

Three other novices received the habit along with Fra
Pio: Fra Anastasio of Roio, who persevered and became
Padre Pio's confidant, and two others who returned to the
world before long for lack of vocation.

We are fortunate in having a document from Padre Pio's
own pen in which, nearly twenty years later, he describes to
one of his spiritual daughters what passed in his soul during
those first days of his novitiate. As a young priest Padre
Pio directed a number of holy people by correspondence.
Two volumes of this correspondence have already appeared
in Italian. They contain the letters he wrote between 1914
and 1922, after which the crowds around his confessional
increased to such an extent that almost all his waking hours
were devoted to this ministry and he had no time for writing.

The document we are about to quote was found after his
death and although it bore no date or indication as to whom
it was addressed, a teacher named Nina Campanile (still
living in San Giovanni Rotondo in 1978) revealed that it was
written to her in November 1922 when Padre Pio was already
living in the friary on Mount Gargano. It sheds some light
on the first days of his novitiate in Morcone immediately
after he had put on the Capuchin habit. He writes:

May Jesus be always with us. I entered on my retreat three days ago
and through God's radiant grace I am arriving at an ever fuller
knowledge of myself and of God's goodness to me and to all of you.
Pray for me to this divine Lover, that he may fulfil in this poor
creature the work of his grace which he has begun. . . My heart has
always been on fire with love for him, my All, and for all men.
Innocently and unwittingly I used to pour out my love on those for
whom I cared, then he who always watched over me would reproach
me in a fatherly manner. . . It was the voice of a kind Father who
intended to detach his son's heart from everything belonging to
earth and the mire, in order that I might devote myself entirely to

him. With sweet and tender words he called me to himself to make me entirely his. Moreover, with what was almost jealousy for his son he often allowed those who were attached to the earth to illtreat me, to shower ungrateful blows on me so that I might understand how false and mistaken was the love which in my innocence I bestowed on creatures. I then understood the dreadful and terrifying picture he had shown me in his infinite mercy (he is referring to the vision of 1903). It was a sight to make the strongest tremble with fear. . . I anxiously called on my good Father who came to my assistance. He seemed to smile and invite me to a different life. He gave me to understand that my safe haven, my peaceful shelter lay in the ranks of the clergy. O my Lord, where can I better serve you than in the cloister, beneath the banner of the *Poverello* of Assisi? Then I felt within me two forces wrestling with each other and tearing my heart asunder: the world that wanted me for itself and God who was calling me to a new life. Dear God! Who can imagine the interior torment I experienced? Although twenty years have passed since then, the mere recollection of that interior combat makes the blood freeze in my veins. You know, O my God, that I always wanted to obey you and that I would rather have died than refuse to answer your call. You know the state of abandonment to which I was reduced at that time and how you stretched out your strong hand and led me firmly to the place to which you had called me. For this I offer infinite praise and thanks to you, O my God. You hid me away from the eyes of all, but even at that time you had entrusted to your son a very great mission, a mission that is known to you and myself alone.

Dear God, my Father! How have I corresponded to such a mission? I hear within me a voice which repeats insistently: "Become holy and make others holy." Help me, my dear daughter, for I know how much Jesus loves you and how deserving you are of this love. Speak to him for me and ask him for the grace to make me a less unworthy son of St Francis, so that I may give good example to my fellow-friars, so that our fervour may continually increase and I may become a perfect Capuchin.[4]

Padre Pio was thirty-five when he penned those lines in 1922. He already bore the bleeding imprints of Christ's passion in his flesh and for four years had been attracting increasing crowds to his humble friary on Mount Gargano. The letter to his spiritual daughter, Nina Campanile, just quoted, is one of the last he was to write, although his ministry was to continue for almost half a century. There are many who deplore the fact that he wrote so little after this date. Yet that one letter furnishes us with the key to his whole life. He hears a voice within him which exhorts him to "become holy and make others holy". It is his earnest desire to be "a less unworthy son of St Francis, to give good example to his confrères, to become a perfect Capuchin". He is aware, moreover, that God has entrusted him with "a very great mission, a mission, dear God, which is known to you and myself alone".

THREE

Preparation for a Mission

Now that Padre Pio is dead, even a cursory glance in retrospect over his extraordinary life leaves us little room to doubt the "very great mission" to which God called him. It was announced to him in the remarkable vision of 1903 on the eve of his entry to the Capuchin order. A period of intense preparation followed, a full fifteen years marked by mysterious events. Then, in September 1918, that mission was sealed, as it were, when he received the bleeding imprint of Christ's wounds in his body. From that day onward it can be said to be a mission to the entire world, a mission that still continues today. St Thérèse of Lisieux declared that she would spend her heaven doing good upon earth. Padre Pio of Pietrelcina said on more than one occasion: "My true mission will begin after my death."

The first stage in the preparation for his mission was his canonical novitiate which lasted a year, at the end of which he pronounced simple vows in the novitiate house of Morcone. He was then sent to the house of studies at Sant'Elia in Pianisi for his philosophy course and later to Serracapriola, Montefusco and Gesualdo to study theology. All of these friaries are situated within the Capuchin province of Foggia which extends over a large area in Southern Italy. The greater part of that four-year period was spent at Sant'-Elia and it was here that he committed himself permanently to God in 1907 by pronouncing his solemn vows of poverty, chastity and obedience in the Capuchin order. Although divine charisms were not lacking during this period, there was nothing unusual to be noted in the life of the Capuchin student who was to become the first stigmatised priest in the history of the Church, if we exclude the fact of his delicate health and his frequent and mysterious high fevers. We really have very little information about his life during those years, except for the testimony of some of his class-

mates and a few reminiscences of his own which he confided
to his confrères in later years.

External ly, everything appeared quite normal. His superiors
and the other students were merely aware that Fra Pio was a
really good friar. Padre Leone of San Giovanni Rotondo, who
studied at Sant'Elia along with him, gives valuable testimony
to this effect. To Padre Alberto, who collected information
from many witnesses at a later stage, Padre Leone related
the following in 1955:

> While we were students in Sant'Elia, Fra Pio always kept to the
> genuine spirit of the novitiate. Quite often when I went to his cell
> to call him, I found him on his knees at the end of his bed, or with
> his face buried in his hands over his books. Sometimes he failed
> to appear in choir for the night office and when I went to call him I
> found him on his knees, deeply immersed in prayer. I never heard
> him complain of the poor food, although the friary could have
> given us something better. He never criticised the actions of the
> superiors and when others did so he either rebuked them or else left
> their company. He never grumbled about the cold which was really
> severe or about the few blankets we were given. However, what
> struck me most about Fra Pio was his love of prayer.[1]

Padre Raffaele recalls how, quite often in September, the
singing of the harvesters in the fields to the north of the
friary would surprise Fra Pio still at prayer from the previous
evening. He prayed at all hours of the day, yet according to
his companions he never went to class unprepared. Padre
Raffaele asserts that in this Fra Pio received special assistance
from God.

Fra Pio and Fra Anastasio arrived together from the
novitiate. Padre Raffaele was an aspirant at Sant'Elia at the
time and it was there that he first made the acquaintance of
Fra Pio. He reports that "from this first meeting I was filled
with great admiration for him because of his exemplary
behaviour". He was in the same house with him for a year
and his summing-up of Fra Pio is: "Young as I was, I didn't
know much about virtue, but I remarked in Fra Pio something which distinguished him from the other students.
Whenever I met him, in the corridors, in choir, in the sacristy, in the garden, he was always humble, recollected and

silent and there was no danger that he would speak an unnecessary word." Another father points out: "He was by no means shy or withdrawn, but affable and approachable and, all his companions were sincerely fond of him."

In January 1972 the cell which was his in Sant'Elia was opened to the public. In other houses of his order he lived only for short periods, so that after the cell in San Giovanni Rotondo which he occupied for over half a century, the little cell in Sant'Elia comes next in importance. There was a big crowd of devotees on that January day in 1972. The cell door bears the following inscription: "In this cell Fra Pio of Pietrelcina studied, prayed, practised the love of God and battled with Satan, from January 1904 to October 1907 and became an exemplary Capuchin." Padre Eusebio Notte, who assisted Padre Pio for five years in San Giovanni Rotondo, spoke for the occasion and illustrated the simple words which appear on the cell door. "He remained here almost four years," he said, "and during that time, by means of his studies but especially through prayer, his awareness of the exceptional mission he was to fulfil matured within him, that mission of which the world is aware today and to which he consecrated himself permanently by the solemn profession of his vows on 27 January 1907."

Although nothing exceptional was to be observed in the young friar at this stage, he himself revealed to his confrères many years later some extraordinary events dating from that period of his late teens.

While I was in Sant'Elia for my philosophy course, my cell was the second last in the corridor which runs behind the church. One night in summer, after Matins, I had both my window and door wide open because of the heat, when I suddenly heard a lot of noise which seemed to come from the cell next my own. I wondered what Fra Anastasio could be doing at such a late hour. I thought he might be praying, so I began to say the Rosary myself. In point of fact, we vied with each other as to who would pray most and I didn't want to be outdone. The noise grew much louder and I was on the point of calling Fra Anastasio when I got a strong smell of sulphur. I went to the window (the windows of our two cells were so close that we could hand books to each other by leaning out) and I tried to call him without raising my voice too much, but there was no reply. At that moment I saw coming in through my door a huge dog breathing smoke from his mouth. I fell back on my bed and heard myself saying: "It's him! It's him!" [the devil]. With that the huge beast sprang out of the window, leaped to the nearby roof and disappeared.

We also have an account from Fra Pio's own pen of some heavenly prodigies which marked those early years of his Capuchin life. The Mother of God appeared to him in Sant'Elia and initiated him into the mission that awaited him as a priest. He himself wrote at the time:

A few days ago something very unusual happened to me. While I was in church with Fra Anastasio at about 11 p.m. (on 18 January 1905), I suddenly found myself in a house far away where a man was dying and a little girl was just being born. Most Holy Mary appeared to me and said: "I entrust this creature to you. She is a precious jewel as yet unpolished. Work on her, polish her, make her as brilliant as possible, because one day I want to adorn myself with her." "How is that possible?" I asked, "when I am still only a poor student and don't even know if I'll have the happiness of becoming a priest? And even if I become a priest, how can I take care of this child when she is so far away?" Then Our Lady said: "Don't doubt. It is she who will come to you, but first of all you will meet her in St Peter's." Then immediately I found myself back in our church.[2]

As we know, Padre Pio was endowed in later years with the remarkable gift of bilocation, the faculty to be present simultaneously in two different places. Here, then, when he was barely eighteen, we have a first instance of this exceptional charism. The visit "to a house far away, where a man was dying and a little girl was being born" is fully confirmed by the subsequent course of events in the life of that little girl, who was born in Udine in the far north of Italy on 18 January 1905 just as her father was leaving this life.

While the girl was growing up she never even heard of Padre Pio and therefore had no idea of what he had written in 1905. When she was 18 she went for the first time to San Giovanni Rotondo, met Padre Pio and learned of the mysterious event which had accompanied her birth.

The story is an intriguing one. Her father was a rich man

and a convinced Freemason and on the night of his death his fellow-Masons were on the watch to make sure that no priest entered the villa. A few hours before the man died, his pious wife, who was praying and weeping, saw the shadowy figure of a priest disappear down the corridor. A dog was howling outside as though to announce his master's passing. The lady went quickly down to the hall, unable to bear the dog's moaning, and she was at once seized with labour pains and gave birth prematurely to a little girl. Some minutes later her husband expired, assisted by a priest and invoking God's pardon in a loud voice. How had the priest entered the villa? The lodge-keeper related that a priest had been waiting outside for some time. The man had persuaded the watchers to let the priest pass when he told them of the birth of the child. "You can prohibit the priest from assisting the dying man," he said, "but you can't stop him from going in to baptise the newborn baby." Thus the priest was admitted, went straight to the dying man's room, heard his confession and assisted him to the end.

After her husband's death this lady moved to Rome where her little daughter, Giovanna, grew up and went to school. During her secondary schooling many of her teachers were unbelievers and she was tormented by doubts about the faith, yet could find no enlightened priest to help her. Then one afternoon in the summer of 1922 she went into St Peter's Basilica intending to go to confession, but the sacristan told her it was closing time and suggested she come back next morning. "At any rate," he said, "it will take me half-an-hour to get around the whole Basilica to lock up, so if you happen to find a priest still there, go to confession." Just then a young Capuchin came into view and went into the second confessional on the left. Giovanna hurried to the confessional and poured out her doubts about some points of dogma which tormented her most. With intelligent and simple words suited to her age the priest enlightened her and dispelled all her doubts. Radiantly happy, she went to the front of the confessional, as Italian penitents often do, to kiss the priest's hand as he came out. But no priest emerged. The sacristan returned and asked her to leave. She told him she had been to confession and was just waiting to thank the confessor. "Signorina," said the man, "there is nobody here." Then he opened the confessional and proved his words. Giovanna was very perplexed and said: "Then where did he go? I didn't see him come out." She pondered deeply on this mysterious happening on her way home.

A year later, with her aunt and some friends she travelled to San Giovanni Rotondo. They waited in the friary corridor where Padre Pio was to pass, Giovanna in the very front row. As Padre Pio came by he looked her straight in the face and said: "I know you. You were born the night your father died." Next day she went to his confessional and he said: "My child, I have waited all these years for you." But the bewildered girl told him: "This is the first time I have come to San Giovanni. You must be mistaking me for some other girl." "No," said Padre Pio, "don't you remember looking for a confessor in St Peter's?" Then he told her frankly that he was the Capuchin who had heard her confession there. He had gone to Rome in bilocation, just as Our Blessed Lady had foretold when she appeared to him in his student days in 1905. Padre Agostino of San Marco in Lamis, who had been Fra Pio's theology professor in 1907 and in later years his confessor, was now (1923) the Guardian in San Giovanni Rotondo. He had kept carefully the account which Fra Pio had written of his bilocation to Udine while still a student. Now, in San Giovanni Rotondo, the Guardian made the acquaintance of this young lady. He showed her the written account of the extraordinary circumstances surrounding her own birth and assured her that the document was genuine. She spoke to Padre Pio about it and he confirmed what the Guardian had told her.

Padre Pio enrolled this girl as a Franciscan tertiary and gave her the name Jacopa. He guided her for years in the spiritual life and she married and brought up a good Christian family. In the last year of his life she heard his voice calling her urgently to the little town on Mount Gargano, where she hastened as soon as she could. When she went to confession, he told her it was the last time, "because I am leaving", he said, referring to his death which took place not many days later. The devout lady told Padre Alberto that she had assisted at Padre Pio's holy death in his own cell, but the friar was quite incredulous. Then she described in minutest detail his cell and all it contained. No photographs had been taken there up to that time and no woman had ever entered the cell. Her description of the scene convinced Padre Alberto. The lady in question gave a sworn statement of all these facts in Manfredonia during the preliminary proceedings for the Cause of Beatification of Padre Pio of Pietrelcina and the document was placed on record.

* * * * *

While he was a philosophy student in Sant'Elia, Fra Pio asked to be sent on the missions. This was in 1905, when Capuchin students were allowed to volunteer for missionary lands. But Fra Pio was informed that from that time onwards only priests would be sent on the missions. He accepted this decision, but we know that he meant to return to the subject as soon as he became a priest. His weak health during the first years of his priesthood made the fulfilment of this desire quite impossible.

In his letters we find an occasional flashback which throws some further light on his student days. When already a young priest he told his spiritual director that divine charisms had not been lacking in those years. Padre Agostino, who had seen him in ecstasy during a brief stay in Venafro friary, wrote to him in his own home in 1915 and asked him to give a sincere account of his interior life. He put several direct questions and asked for a frank answer to each one. The first question was: "When did Jesus begin to favour you with heavenly visions?" On 15 October 1915 Padre Pio replied: "You want to know when Jesus began to favour his poor creature with heavenly visions. If I am not mistaken, these must have begun not long after the novitiate." In Sant'Elia, most probably.

Having pronounced his solemn vows in 1907, Fra Pio

continued his studies in various houses of his province. In December 1908 he received minor orders and the subdiaconate. During this period his delicate health obliged his superiors to send him several times to his own home, where the air seemed to revive him. In May 1909 a further deterioration in his health obliged him to interrupt his theological studies. In the hope that the change of air would again restore him, his doctors and superiors decided to send him once more to his native town. They hoped that a brief spell there would be sufficient, but God had other designs and, with the exception of a few short intervals, he was to remain until February 1916 in Pietrelcina, a period of almost seven years. During all that time his habitual state was one of precarious health, the causes of which nobody succeeded in diagnosing. To his doctors he was an unknown quantity and his spiritual directors were equally baffled. This whole period of his life is, in fact, shrouded in mystery and his official biographers seem unable to offer any plausible explanation. Certain it is that during those years spent at home his interior life was most intense and he made giant strides on the way to perfection. Perhaps this long and painful period spent in comparative isolation from his brethren can be seen as a prolonged retreat, as it were, in which the soul of this modern mystic was to be completely purified in the furnace of suffering, in preparation for the "very great mission" which awaited him in the years that followed.

FOUR

Back to Pietrelcina

There is a village not many miles north of Venice which sees a constant stream of visitors to the humble home in which Pope St Pius X was born and reared. This great pope, who was elected on 9 August 1903 while Padre Pio was a novice in Morcone friary, and who died of grief a few days after the outbreak of World War I, carried the fine qualities of his kinsfolk of the staunchly Catholic Veneto region into his public life. After his canonisation in 1954 the name of his little hometown, Riese, was officially changed to Riese San Pio X (Riese of St Pius X). Much more recently another little rural spot in the equally fervent Catholic area of Bergamo came into the headlines: Sotto il Monte, the birthplace of Pope John XXIII which in turn has become a place of pilgrimage. If we want to know a person thoroughly it is natural to visit the places in which he lived. History is not made without the aid of geography.

Today, while the cause for beatification and canonisation of Padre Pio is in the hands of the competent authorities, many devout pilgrims on their way to his tomb in San Giovanni Rotondo visit the environment in which his early life was spent. Here, in the pleasant setting of a valley from which the industrious population draws its livelihood, the church, the simple home of the Forgione family and the remains of a famous elm tree are silent witnesses to the wonderful things God was pleased to accomplish in the soul of an ailing young friar whose whole being was consumed by love for his Lord: consolations and spiritual joys, to be sure, but also atrocious sufferings which he himself described as comparable only to the pains of hell; continual combats with the devil; visions of Jesus and Mary and the constant tangible presence of his guardian angel.

God's designs on this Capuchin student were undoubtedly mysterious. The symptoms of a hacking cough, severe chest-

31

pains and extremely high temperatures which emerged in his final year of theology, gave rise to the fear that he was affected by tuberculosis, although several physicians at various stages of his life excluded this possibility in the most absolute manner. While anxious to give Fra Pio every chance to recover in his native air, his superiors had a further motive for separating him from the other students, for they feared his illness was contagious. Hence we find him, to his deep chagrin, segregated from community life and obliged to live at home. The Forgione home was of very modest dimensions, but his parents rented another room quite near, a quiet place where Fra Pio could pray and study undisturbed. In this little room, high up in an old tower which is approached by a steep flight of steps, the young friar spent much of his time in those years of enforced exile from his community.It was here that he penned many of the letters which describe so graphically his spiritual experiences. When the season was warmer he spent long hours in the open air, in an isolated spot on the family farm while the others worked in the fields.

Neither Fra Pio himself nor his superiors had any idea of the length of time that was to elapse before he would return to normal Capuchin life. As the months passed and his health showed no signs of improvement, Padre Benedetto, his Provincial, became very dissatisfied with this situation. We sense the drama of those months as we read the correspondence which passed between them. Fra Pio had been sent to his home in May 1909. On 2 January 1910 Padre Benedetto wrote to him:

> What the divine plan is in wanting you almost invariably in your own home, I do not know. However, I adore this plan and confidently hope that the problem will solve itself. If your health is improving to a noticeable extent in your native air, stay there and pray the good God that he may at least make you fit to study a little and do what is necessary to be promoted to the priesthood.

A regulation issued by the Congregation for Religious in 1909 stated that in particular cases ecclesiastical studies followed privately were valid for ordination to the priesthood. In the weeks that followed, Fra Pio referred frequently in his letters to his burning desire to be ordained a priest. He was racked by high fevers at intervals and suffered continually from severe chest pains. However, when he felt a little stronger and was able to walk, he took lessons in theology from a priest, always with his cherished goal in view.

At last, on 1 July, the necessary dispensation for his ordination was obtained from the Holy See. On 6 July the Provincial wrote to inform him that he might be ordained early in August and that he must go to Morcone friary to learn the rubrics. With his usual prompt obedience, Fra Pio travelled the twenty-five miles to Morcone with a friar who had been sent to accompany him, but no sooner had he reached the friary than he became violently ill and was confined to bed in a state of extreme weakness. He returned almost immediately to Pietrelcina. In a letter written shortly afterwards, his Provincial expressed his regret and a certain perplexity that "God does not allow you to live in that cloister to which he himself has with great condescension called you. Perhaps he wants you to be an exile in the world so that you may place all your hope and pleasure in him alone." However, he arranged for Fra Pio to be instructed in the rubrics in his own parish and for the ordination to take place in Benevento, only a few miles away.

Padre Pio was ordained by Most Rev. Paolo Schinosi in Benevento Cathedral on 10 August 1910 and on the following Sunday, 14 August, sang high Mass in his own parish. In his personal notes, as a souvenir of his ordination he wrote: "Jesus, my heart's desire and my life, today as I raise you up in trembling hands in a mystery of love, may I be, *with* you, the way, the truth and the life for the world, and *for* you a holy priest, a perfect victim."

His health was quite precarious and there could be no question of his return to conventual life. He continued to give a faithful account of his spiritual life in his letters to the Provincial who was also his spiritual director. In addition to his bodily sufferings he was beset with spiritual torments. His letters during this period are full of loving resignation to all the trials the Lord was pleased to send him. He felt greatly in need of wise counsel and support in his trials and

Padre Benedetto responded with enlightening words which consoled and comforted him. He was constantly assailed by diabolical temptations and while he accepted without a murmur his severe physical ailments, he desired to be set free from these temptations for fear of offending God. On 29 September 1910 he wrote:

> It is true that I am suffering, but I am very happy in this state, for you [Padre Benedetto] have assured me that it does not mean that God has abandoned me but rather shows the delicacy of his exquisite love. I hope the Lord is pleased to accept my sufferings in satisfaction for the innumerable times I have offended him. After all, what is my suffering in comparison to what I deserve for my sins?

In this letter he also told Padre Benedetto that for some time past he had felt the need to offer himself to the Lord as a victim for sinners and for the souls in purgatory.

> This desire has been growing continually in my heart and has now become what I would call a strong passion. I have, in fact, made this offering to the Lord several times, beseeching him to pour out on me the punishments prepared for sinners and for souls in a state of purgation, even increasing them a hundredfold . . . but I would now like to make this offering to the Lord in obedience to you . . . I am sure you will have no difficulty in granting me this permission.

This is the first reference to the victim state to be found in his letters, a subject that is to recur frequently in the years spent in Pietrelcina separated from his beloved Capuchin community. His director fully understood his generous desires and granted him permission to offer himself as a victim. "Make the offering of which you speak," he wrote, "and it will be most acceptable to the Lord. Stretch out your arms on your own cross and by offering to the Father the sacrifice of yourself in union with our most loving Saviour, suffer, groan and pray for the wicked ones of the earth and for the poor souls in the next life who are so deserving of our compassion in their patient and unspeakable sufferings" (1-12-1910).

Month succeeded month and spring arrived once more. Padre Pio had now been a full two years "in exile" from his community. He continued to open his heart to Padre Benedetto in his letters, from which we can follow at least in a dim manner the marvellous action of God in his soul. He was not yet twenty-five but his prayer-life was already far advanced. Physical torments were continual and, as he said himself, "spiritual battles keep pace with my bodily sufferings". He was constantly afflicted with severe headaches and it cost him a great effort to write. He feared that the devil was trying to prevent him from communicating with his director. He meditated constantly on Jesus' torments and this caused him to suffer intensely, but "this is a suffering which does me good", he wrote, "and I enjoy an inexplicable peace and tranquillity" (29-3-1911). As his zeal for souls grew white-hot, he yearned to minister to them directly. In April of that same year he asked his Provincial to grant him the faculty to hear men's confessions during Holy Week. But Padre Benedetto did not see his way to allow this. "It would be very detrimental to your health," he wrote in reply, "and perhaps also to your peace of soul. If you were well enough to hear confessions you would not be at home and getting special treatment. If Providence is pleased to destine you for this ministry, which is particularly heavy for those with chest trouble, he will first have to give you the health you lack."

At intervals during the months that followed, Padre Pio renewed his request to be allowed to hear confessions, at least on some special occasions in order to help the local priests, but the Provincial continued to refuse. So this extraordinary friar, already living in close union with God and offering himself daily in the midst of unspeakable sufferings as a victim for souls, this frail young priest who was to become one of the most remarkable confessors of our century and to reconcile countless sinners to God and lead many more to heights of holiness, was denied the faculty to hear confessions. This in itself was for him an additional most painful trial during those years of isolation in Pietrelcina.

In June 1911 Padre Pio became more seriously ill. He wrote to tell the Provincial of his turn for the worse and of his desire to see a specialist. Padre Benedetto's reply might seem harsh.

> Since you long to be dissolved in order to be in Christ, I am not
> sorry to hear that you are worse . . . I consider it useless for you to
> consult doctors. I am convinced that your sufferings are directly
> and expressly willed by God and that there is no remedy. But if
> you do not find my judgment acceptable, then follow the advice
> of the experts. I would like very much to see you in community.
> Am I to be denied this consolation for ever?

Padre Benedetto was a master in the spiritual life and was
aware by this time that he was dealing with no ordinary soul.
As their correspondence continues, the mystical ascent of
the young Capuchin emerges plainly and Padre Benedetto's
ability to direct his exceptional young disciple is equally
evident.

In the late summer of 1911 Padre Pio mentioned the
stigmata for the first time. In a letter dated 8 September he
wrote to Padre Benedetto:

> Yesterday evening something happened to me which I can neither
> explain nor understand. In the centre of the palms of my hands a
> red patch appeared, about the size of a *centesimo* [a small coin,
> about half an inch in diameter] and accompanied by sharp pain.
> The pain was more acute in the left hand and it still persists. I also
> feel some pain in the soles of my feet. This phenomenon has been
> repeated several times for almost a year now, but for some time
> past it had not occurred. Do not be upset by the fact that this is the
> first time I have mentioned it, for I was invariably overcome by
> abominable shame. If you only knew what it costs to tell you about
> it now!

He had been more than two years at home when Padre
Agostino, his former professor, began to correspond with
him also, and from the beginning of 1912 we find Padre
Pio writing to him fairly often, while he continues to give
an account of his spiritual life to Padre Benedetto. Some time
later, when misunderstandings arose between Padre Pio and
the Provincial, mainly due to the former's protracted absence
from community and the Provincial's desire to have him back
in the cloister, Padre Agostino became the mediator and wrote
consoling and helpful letters to the young Capuchin to whom
Padre Benedetto's lack of understanding had become a
grievous trial.

In the spring of 1912 we find some of Padre Agostino's letters to Padre Pio written in French and now and then Padre Pio replied in the same language. Padre Agostino had taught French in the seminary, but Padre Pio had never studied this language at all. Yet he read with ease the letters he received in French. Some months later, when Padre Agostino wrote to him in Greek, he translated easily from this language also, although he did not even know the Greek alphabet! Padre Agostino had already guessed that his young correspondent received supernatural assistance in this matter and, in point of fact, when Padre Pio was asked to explain his ability to read French and Greek, he replied quite simply that his guardian angel acted as his interpreter. In later life, during his arduous ministry as a confessor and spiritual guide to people from many parts of the world, we find many well-documented instances of his use of this "gift of tongues" which first emerged during his enforced exile in Pietrelcina.

During these years spent in his own home, although Padre Pio kept very much to himself, the townspeople began to have an inkling of the remarkable life of this emaciated young friar. He was always friendly and smiling when they met him, but he acted with great reserve. His physical appearance in itself was sufficient to make people wonder. He had a good word for everyone, a gentle reproof for those who were too free in their speech and for anyone who was disinclined to respect the Lord's day. The women in Rione Castello took care not to be caught ironing or mending when he passed by on a Sunday. "Look out," someone would say, "here comes Padre Pio!" He was fond of the children and spent many an hour teaching them their prayers and catechism. In Lent he used to bring all the youngsters of his own district to his home and patiently teach them the hymns and chants for Holy Week and Easter.

The people of Pietrelcina suspected that they had a saint in their midst and they loved to have him with them. They felt he was theirs and someone of whom to be proud. Padre Agostino used to visit him from time to time and some of the townsfolk began to fear he would take Padre Pio away from them. A man challenged the older friar one day with the following words: "So you want to carry off our *santari-ello?* Well, we'll break your neck if you attempt it!" On another occasion they really threatened Padre Agostino's physical safety and he escaped unhurt only by the timely arrival of the parish priest and Padre Pio himself.

Towards the end of 1913 Padre Benedetto's letters clearly show his dissatisfaction at Padre Pio's prolonged absence from community life. He had by that time been four-and-a-half years in his own home. On 7 November 1913 the Provincial wrote: "When will you decide to come back to us? Even if your return to religious life meant dying sooner there would be nothing wrong, for certainly no one should leave religious life for the sake of living longer!" A few weeks later (17 December) he returned to the subject: "When do you intend to return to the friary? By this time you have had experience of your native air and it is evident that it sustains but does not cure you. I repeat what I have already told you . . . that I see nothing extraordinary or contrary to the divine will in a return to religious life, even with the firm conviction that you would become worse . . . I would really like you to go to Morcone to act as assistant novice-master." Padre Pio was deeply distressed. His health at the time had deteriorated still further. He replied on 20 December: "You who know me thoroughly can imagine how gladly I would fly to community life, but since my illness is growing more and more serious and I can hardly drag myself around, I should be a burden and a nuisance to the community and my end would only be hastened." He reminded his Provincial that the Superior General, who viewed with disfavour such a long stay in his own home, had remarked that it would be better to apply for a Brief of Exclaustration and become a secular priest. Padre Pio appealed to Padre Benedetto to obtain this document from the Holy See on his behalf, "although it breaks my heart," he wrote, "to be obliged to take this step".

In the weeks that followed there was a frequent exchange of letters between Padre Pio and Padre Agostino. The latter urged Padre Pio not to insist on obtaining the Brief but to go to Morcone as Padre Benedetto desired. Padre Pio complied with this suggestion but with disastrous results. Just as on several previous occasions, when he had hastened to obey and had returned to the friary indicated by his superiors, he fell dangerously ill. This time, after five days he had to return to Pietrelcina.

During spring 1914 the Capuchins held their General Chapter and a new Superior General was elected. This was Padre Venantius of Lisle-en-Rigault, who visited the Foggia Province in May of the same year. Padre Pio was extremely ill at the time and was unable to travel in order to meet his new Superior General with whom his exceptional situation had been discussed. A full year was to pass, a year of particular trials for Padre Pio, before a solution was found for his case. Finally, on 7 March 1915 Padre Benedetto wrote to inform Padre Pio that His Holiness Pope Benedict XV had granted him "the faculty requested to remain outside the cloister as long as necessary, while continuing to wear the habit of his order". In his reply dated 11 March, Padre Pio poured out his gratitude for this favour, which meant that he was not to become a secular priest but could continue to follow the Capuchin rule which he had embraced with such ardour and generosity twelve years earlier. He expressed the hope that he would be granted "at least the grace to die in that place to which God in his immense fatherly goodness called me", adding that "this sweet hope sustains me and enables me to go on living". With his typical ardent generosity he went on at once to say that "as Jesus has not allowed me to devote myself entirely to my beloved Mother Province, I have offered myself to the Lord as a victim for her spiritual needs".

Padre Pio was still in Pietrelcina when Italy entered World War I, an event which created enormous difficulties for his Capuchin province, as many of the friars were called up for military service. He himself was summoned to appear at the local recruiting office and was sent on to Naples. Less than two weeks later he was home on convalescent leave for a year. In August 1917, when he was already back in his friary, he was called up once more. Despite his very precarious state of health he was assigned to the Tenth Medical Corps in Naples and was thus obliged to spend several months in uniform; sometimes he was even deprived of the opportunity of saying Mass. His letters to Padre Benedetto and Padre Agostino during those months reveal the torture he endured in the environment of a military barracks.

His last letter from Pietrelcina is dated 15 February 1916. The mysterious design which had kept him for nearly seven years in his own home had evidently been fulfilled and we now find him in St Anne's Friary in Foggia. From this city, where the oppressive heat endangered his health once more, he was transferred to San Giovanni Rotondo, just twenty-five miles away, where his "great mission" emerged distinctly and continued for over half a century.

FIVE

Mystical Ascent

"I believe that the true story of Padre Pio's spiritual life is to be found in his *Letters,* of which the first volume appeared very recently.[1] Those who want to understand Padre Pio of Pietrelcina, rather than reading a biography written by some-one else ought to read his *Letters. "* This statement was made by Joseph Cardinal Siri, Archbishop of Genoa, in an address to a large meeting of Padre Pio's devotees assembled in that city in September 1973 to commemorate the fifth anniversary of his death. The Cardinal was referring to the young friar's correspondence with his spiritual directors during the years of his enforced absence from his community.

Another prelate, Most Rev. Mgr Paolo Carta, formerly Bishop of Foggia and at present Archbishop of Sassari (Sardinia) stated:

> On reading the first volume of his *Letters,* which contains his corres-pondence with his spiritual directors from 1910 to 1922, I was deeply impressed and moved. Although I already held Padre Pio in great esteem I should never have imagined that his union with God and his prayer life had reached those sublime heights of mysticism which I admired in St Teresa of Avila. For me this was a wonderful discovery. I rejoiced to think that I had known him, had made my confession to him, had taken part in great events of his life and had embraced him many times. In his intimate relations with God he reached the summit of transforming union and mystical experience.[2]

In those very early days of his priesthood, during which he wrote the letters to which both of these prelates refer, Padre Pio climbed the "mountain of perfection" with rapid strides. It is not given to many souls to progress so quickly on the path of mysticism. Before he was thirty years of age Padre Pio had already "reached the summit of transforming union and mystical experience". The best way to trace his mystical ascent is to let him speak for himself, in the letters he wrote during that period. At most we add an occasional explanatory comment borrowed from the introduction to the first volume of his *Letters,* where an attempt is made to classify the phenomena to which he refers.[3] Adopting the generally accepted terminology in this field, his biographers speak of *impulses or transports of love, divine touches, strokes and wounds of love, transverberation* and *stigmatisation.*

Padre Pio's love for God was so strong that it sometimes exploded without warning in surprising transitory effects which were reflected in some way in his whole person. What the specialists describe as impulses of love were transports inspired by the intensity of his love for God. He yearned with all his heart to correspond to divine love and when he found himself unable to satisfy this desire he either fainted or burst into tears. The loving impulse, while increasing his spiritual powers, produced the effects of a genuine illness and his body became quite weak. Acute pain was counterbalanced by ineffable spiritual delight. He yearned intensely to be united with God for ever.[4] On 30 January 1915 he wrote:

I feel my heart and my whole interior permeated by the flames of an immense fire. Along with the atrocious agony caused by these flames, my soul experiences an exceeding sweetness which makes me burn with love for God. I feel annihilated and I find no place in which to hide from this gift of the divine Master. I am ill with an illness of the heart and I can bear it no longer. It seems as if the thread of life is about to snap at any moment, yet that moment never comes. My dear Father [he is writing to Padre Benedetto], how sad is the state of a soul which God has wounded by his love. For pity's sake, pray to the Lord that he may put an end to my days, for I just haven't the courage to go on in such a state. I see no other remedy unless that of being consumed once and for all by these flames which burn yet never consume me. Do not think that it is merely my soul which experiences this martyrdom. My body also, even though indirectly, shares in it to a very great extent. While this divine operation continues, my body is becoming utterly powerless.

Divine touches, a delightful contact which God produces on "the point of the soul," at the "apex of the spirit" are described in the writings of many of the great mystics. These touches are sometimes referred to as *substantial* because they seem to take place between two substances. Such experiences are not reached by human efforts, but are a free gift of the divine benevolence. In Padre Pio's letters we find a description of a fusion of hearts and a substantial touch or kiss of love.[5] On 18 April 1912 he wrote to Padre Benedetto:

There are some things which cannot be translated into human language without losing their deep and heavenly meaning. This morning the heart of Jesus and my own — allow me to use the expression — were fused. No longer were two hearts beating, but one alone. My own heart had disappeared as a drop of water is lost in the sea. My joy was so intense and profound that I could not contain myself. My dear Father, man cannot understand that when paradise is poured into a heart, this afflicted, exiled and weak mortal heart cannot bear it without weeping. The very joy that filled my heart was what made me weep for so long.

On 8 March 1916 he wrote to his spiritual director:

Once only did I feel in the secret depths of my soul something so delicate that I cannot describe it. First of all, without seeing anything, my soul felt his presence. Then, let me put it this way, he came so close to my soul that I felt his touch, exactly as happens — to give you a faint idea — when one body touches another. I can say no more about this. I can only confess that I was seized at first with the greatest fear, which changed a little later to heavenly exultation . . . I cannot tell you whether, when that happened, I was aware or not of still being in the body. God alone knows this. I am unable to say anything more to give you an understanding of this important occurrence.

Two years later, on 27 July 1918, we find him describing a further experience of this divine touch.

Here is how it came about. I call to mind that on the morning of Corpus Christi, a breath of life was offered to me during the Offertory of the Mass. I cannot give you the remotest idea of what occurred within me in that fleeting moment. I felt utterly shaken, I was filled with extreme terror and I very nearly died. There followed a complete calm such as I had never before experienced. All this terror, agitation and calm one after the other was not caused by the sight of anything, but by something I felt touching the most profound and secret depths of my soul. I can say no more as to how it really happened.

The intensity of divine love which develops gradually and destroys everything opposed to full and total transformation into the Beloved produces another marvellous effect which the mystics call strokes and wounds of love. Some of these are purely spiritual and interior, while others are manifested externally. Padre Pio, who was wounded in both ways, described them vividly and realistically, although he spoke, as usual, of his inability to give an accurate description of such things.[6] At intervals, from 1912 onwards, he described the "interior strokes and wounds of love" to which he was subjected. On 26 August 1912 he wrote:

> I was in church last Friday making my thanksgiving after Mass when I suddenly felt my heart pierced by an arrow of such living and ardent fire that I thought I should die. I have no adequate words to convey to you the intensity of that flame. The soul that is a victim of these consolations is struck dumb. It seemed to me as if some invisible force had plunged me entirely into this fire. I had experienced these transports of love before, but on the other occasions the fire was less intense. This time a second more would have been sufficient to separate my soul from my body.

On 24 January 1915 his description of an interior wound of love was even more graphic:

> The agony I am experiencing is so great that I do not believe I shall suffer more at the supreme hour of death. I feel that someone is plunging a knife into me time after time, a knife with a very sharp point and as if it were emitting fire, which passes through my heart and searches its very depths. Then with all his might this person pulls it out, to repeat a little later the same operation. All this, as these knife-thrusts are repeated, causes my soul to blaze up more and more with exceeding love of God.

The mystical writers describe the wounds of love as being deeper and more lasting than what they describe as strokes of love. Morover, the former are manifested in some external manner, either by a physical piercing of the heart (transverberation) or else by appearing in some parts of the body, such as hands, feet or side (stigmatisation). St Teresa of Avila experienced the extraordinary mystical phenomenon of transverberation, sometimes called "the seraph's assault".

According to the classic doctrine of St John of the Cross, "the soul inflamed with love of God is interiorly attacked by a seraph" who sets it on fire by "piercing it through with a fiery dart". The soul thus wounded is filled with a delightful sweetness.[7] Padre Pio of Pietrelcina received this extraordinary grace on 5 August 1918. He was already nearing the summit of the mystical mountain which he had begun to climb from the moment of his entry into the Capuchin order. The letter in which he related this happening to his spiritual director is one of the most extraordinary in the whole volume and the terms in which he describes it are not far removed from St Teresa's description of the same phenomenon. Padre Pio wrote, on 21 August 1918:

> By virtue of obedience I have made up my mind to reveal to you what happened to me on the evening of the 5th and for the entire day on the 6th of this month . . . I was hearing our boys' confessions on the evening of the 5th when I was suddenly filled with great terror at the sight of a heavenly person who presented himself to my mental gaze. He held in his hand a kind of weapon, like a very long sharp-pointed blade which seemed to emit fire. At the very instant in which I saw all this, that person hurled the weapon into my soul with all his might. I cried out with difficulty and thought I was dying. I asked the boy to leave because I felt ill and no longer had the strength to continue. This agony lasted uninterruptedly until the morning of the 7th. I cannot tell you how much I suffered during this period of anguish. Even my entrails were torn and ruptured by that weapon and nothing was spared. From that day on I have been mortally wounded. I feel in the depths of my soul a wound that is always open and causes me continual agony.

In reply to this dramatic account of the transverberation, his spiritual director, a genuine master of the spiritual life, wrote him a beautiful and reassuring letter. "All that is happening to you", he said, "is the effect of love . . . Your trial is not even a purgation, but a suffering union. The fact of the wound completes your passion just as it completed the Passion of your Beloved on the Cross . . . Kiss the hand which has transfixed you and cherish tenderly this wound which is the seal of love."

Padre Pio's mystical ascent was to culminate in the grace of the bleeding stigmata only a few weeks later. His letters during the period leading up to that memorable date can be compared to the finest pages in the annals of Christian mysticism. He is on fire with love, wounded by love, consumed by the desire to be united with his divine Lover, but at the same time his soul is plunged in the depths of the "dark night". He undergoes unspeakable torments, spiritual and physical. Satan seems to him to be getting the upper hand and on 4 June 1918, he fears he has lost his God for ever. "Tears are my daily bread. I have gone astray and have lost you, but shall I find you again? Or have I lost you for ever? Have you condemned me to live for all eternity far from your countenance? My supreme Good, where are you? I no longer know you or find you. My God, my God, why have you forsaken me?" He appeals desperately to Padre Benedetto to come to the rescue. He is "lost in the unknown". He no longer understands anything and fears he has been abandoned by God for ever. "I clutch or try to clutch at obedience, but even this seems to elude me." Then he asks his director's blessing and concludes with the most touching phrase in all his letters: "I never cease to offer myself for you to the God whom I have lost."

On 19 June we find him writing: "The animal in me shows up in all its abominable reality. All the beauty of grace has been torn out of my soul, and when one is left completely to oneself one comes close to the level of the brute beast . . . I approach the altar with disgust and repugnance for the monstrousness and foulness that accompanies me." Moreover, he is tortured by the thought that he may be deceived and may be "manifesting as true what might not be true". He refers continually to his state as "confinement in a harsh dark prison from which there is no escape". He believes he is being punished by God's justice for his infidelities. On 27 July he feels he is "contemptible in God's eyes and deserves to be cast off, rejected and abandoned by him". Yet it is in the midst of these torments that he experiences the "divine touch" which he describes in the same letter. He is continually beset by grievous temptations.

Satan is constantly at my side with his tireless promptings. I make every effort to fight him, but I realise that I am powerless to free myself by a strong act of my will. I am afraid he is gaining some advantage, because he is always around me and returns continually to the attack. The opposing forces are advancing, dear Father, and they strike at the very centre of my defence. Holy obedience, which was the last prop left to keep the tottering fortress from falling, seems to be yielding like the rest before the Satanic invasion" (5 September).

Then, significantly, he is silent for over a month, and it is during this period, on 20 September 1918, that his sufferings and his mystical journey culminate in the stigmata, the inflicting on his frail and tortured body of the bleeding wounds of Christ's passion.

In Padre Pio's case, transverberation was the prelude to stigmatisation. The former is considered as a grace which sanctifies the soul on which it is bestowed, while the gift of the stigmata is of a charismatic nature granted by God for the benefit of others, although it is the complement, the outward sign and projection of the wound within the soul.[8] Padre Pio had experienced the first symptoms of stigmatisation as early as 1910, very soon after his ordination to the priesthood. As he told his spiritual director, the pain of the wounds continued although the outward signs soon disappeared. In 1912 he wrote to Padre Agostino, his confessor at that time: "From Thursday evening until Saturday and also on Tuesday there is a painful tragedy for me. My heart, hands and feet seem to be pierced through by a sword. I experience great pain on this account." The prodigy was completed on 20 September 1918 and from that time onwards until the last year of his life the bleeding wounds were always visible. He was most reluctant to speak about such an extraordinary favour, but after repeated requests from his spiritual director he overcame his enormous repugnance and sent him, 22 October 1918, a sincere account of the event which marked a decisive stage in his earthly existence and set the seal on his extraordinary priestly ministry.

What can I tell you in answer to your questions concerning my crucifixion? Dear God! What embarrassment and humiliation I suffer by being obliged to explain what you have done to this wretched creature! On the morning of the 20th of last month, after I had celebrated Mass I yielded to a peacefulness similar to a sweet sleep. All the internal and external senses and the very faculties of my soul were immersed in an indescribable stillness. Absolute silence surrounded and invaded me. I was suddenly filled with great peace and abandonment which effaced everything else and caused a lull in the turmoil. All this happened in a flash. Meanwhile I saw before me a mysterious person similar to the one I had seen on the evening of 5 August, but this time his hands and feet and side were dripping blood. The sight frightened me and what I felt at that moment cannot be described. I thought I should die and indeed I should have died if the Lord had not intervened and strengthened my heart which was about to burst out of my chest.

The vision disappeared and I became aware that my own hands and feet and side were dripping blood. Imagine the agony I experienced and continue to experience almost every day! The heart wound bleeds continually, especially from Thursday evening until Saturday. Dear Father, I am dying of pain because of the wound and the resulting embarrassment. I am afraid I shall bleed to death if the Lord does not hear my heartfelt supplication to relieve me of this condition . . . I will raise my voice and will not stop imploring him until in his mercy he takes away, not the wound or the pain, which is impossible because I wish to be inebriated with pain, but these outward signs which cause me such embarrassment and unbearable humiliation.

SIX

His Spiritual Director

God himself leads souls to holiness, but he ordinarily makes use of human instruments to achieve his purpose. He usually places close to the chosen one a holy person who becomes the counsellor, the "spiritual director", the one who is to make God's will clear in all the circumstances of life. Spiritual direction may be defined as the application of the science of the spiritual life to a particular soul, the assistance without which it would be extremely difficult to advance towards perfection. In point of fact, if we take up the life of any saint we invariably find somebody close to him who guides him along the path to holiness. One of the conditions for successful spiritual guidance is that the disciple should have unlimited confidence in his counsellor and it therefore stands to reason that the director himself must be really holy, filled with zeal for God's glory and for the salvation of souls and fully acquainted with the ascetical and mystical life. He must, moreover, be a docile instrument of the Holy Spirit and know how to recognise the workings of grace in the soul he guides.

Obviously, God intended to lead Padre Pio of Pietrelcina to a high degree of holiness and to endow him with extra-ordinary mystical and charismatic gifts. It was therefore necessary that he should have by his side a priest adequately prepared for the task of directing him. His biographers speak of his spiritual "directors" and in fact his correspondence from Pietrelcina was carried on with *two* Capuchins in whom he confided. But according to many confidences made to his confrères in later life, he had only *one* spiritual guide, Padre Benedetto of San Marco in Lamis, who fulfilled this role over a number of years, until the young friar was deprived of this support which meant so much to him. The other priest in whom he confided during those crucial years was his former theology professor, Padre Agostino, also of San Marco in

Lamis. A great many years later when Padre Pio was asked if he had a spiritual director, he replied: "I had, and it was Padre Benedetto, but since they took him away from me I have had none."

St Teresa of Avila, now a Doctor of the Church, was fond of pointing out to her nuns the need for adequate spiritual guidance, the need to speak of one's spiritual state with holy and learned people. "It should be possible to find a number of people who combine learning with spirituality", she remarks, and goes on to insist on the need for *learned* directors. "Learning is a great help in throwing light upon everything", she tells us.[1] Padre Benedetto Nardella, the man who exercised such a deep influence on Padre Pio during the early years of his priesthood, was a learned as well as a genuinely holy man, a man of prayer and austere virtue. Highly intelligent and practical, he was well versed in the mystical life and fully acquainted with Catholic hagiography. He was born in the little town of San Marco in Lamis, only a few miles from San Giovanni Rotondo, and was fifteen years older than Padre Pio. While pursuing his secondary schooling in Foggia he heard the call to religious life and he put on the Capuchin habit in the novitiate of Morcone which Padre Pio was to enter a dozen years later.

Padre Benedetto distinguished himself as a student and was ordained to the priesthood in 1898. He came out on top in a competitive examination within his order for the chair of philosophy and physics and soon became a most successful teacher in the scholasticates of the Capuchin province of Foggia. His outstanding qualities as a teacher and his unusual erudition made him popular with his students, who afterwards maintained affectionate relations with him. He was a talented writer, painter and sculptor. He wrote a number of ascetical books in his later years and contributed constantly to Capuchin magazines devoted to the third order and the missions. He was sought as a preacher all over Southern and Central Italy and was extremely active in spreading the Third Order of St Francis, but he is best remembered for the numerous letters by which he counselled people seeking perfection, either in religion or in secular life. He fashioned souls as an artist works on marble or wood, with the skill of a master. As Provincial from 1909 to 1919 he laboured tirelessly for the spiritual and intellectual development of his province. During World War I he suffered intensely when more than sixty of his friars were called up for military service and the friaries were almost emptied. He had the consolation of being able to keep the "Seraphic Seminary" open in San Giovanni Rotondo during those difficult years and in this his closest collaborator was Padre Pio, who was for a short time vice-rector and for a longer period spiritual director of the Capuchin aspirants there.

Padre Benedetto and Padre Pio first met on 25 April 1903 in Morcone, where Padre Pio was making his novitiate. Padre Benedetto was the latter's teacher during the school year 1905-6 in San Marco la Catola and in that friary examined him in philosophy in September 1907. It was he who, as Provincial Superior, granted Padre Pio permission in January 1910 to remain in his own home on account of his delicate health. Later in the same year he informed Padre Pio of the dispensation which had been obtained for his priestly ordination, as he had not yet reached the required age. He made several attempts in the months that followed to reinstate Padre Pio in community life, but when it was evident that God disposed otherwise Padre Benedetto obtained leave for him from the Holy See, through the Superior General, to remain at home in Pietrelcina while continuing to wear the Capuchin habit. Padre Pio had already been confiding in Padre Agostino, but when he came to know Padre Benedetto and caught a glimpse of this priest's exceptional ability, he chose him as his spiritual guide, although he continued to confide frequently in Padre Agostino.

Padre Benedetto realised immediately that he was dealing with no ordinary soul. He acted with prudence and caution and sought information from others about the young friar and his interior life. Then, with Padre Pio's consent, he asked for all the correspondence that had passed between himself and Padre Agostino. When he was perfectly convinced that what was happening in Padre Pio's soul was due to the genuine action of God, he took him in hand completely and guided

him in masterful fashion. He was a strict director and somewhat dictatorial. He never indulged in sentimentalism even
when, in particular circumstances and with regard to some
spiritual or psychological states, his words became more
human and confidential. In spite of some passing misunderstandings, Padre Benedetto always enjoyed esteem, veneration
and absolute assent on the part of Padre Pio. He was his true
teacher and his sure guide in the ways of the spirit.

The letters written by Padre Benedetto to Padre Pio have
received less publicity than Padre Pio's letters to him. Now
that the collection of their correspondence has appeared in
English[2] it is easier to assess Padre Benedetto's influence on
the spirituality of his disciple. As a really able director he
desired to be informed in detail of all that went on in the
interior life of the young friar. When the latter had written
to him about some revelations or locutions, he replied on 15
June 1913 asking him for a complete account of these things:
"I should like to know something clear as to what you seem
to understand during the supernatural revelations or locutions
which you mention. Even if it is not possible for you to
describe them exactly, write down what you know and can
tell me about them. In these matters we must proceed
cautiously and not take for gold everything that glitters."
He was fully aware of the danger of illusion in such matters.
Here is a page, written to Padre Pio on 10 April 1915, which
is typical of his wise direction:

> When I cast suspicion on one interior locution I did not intend to
> induce you to doubt all locutions and your general state of soul. A
> great many locutions and revelations can be false, but it does not
> necessarily follow that the soul is deceived in everything. It has often
> happened that the most enlightened and holy souls have been subject
> to error or to deception by the devil, yet they are venerated on our
> altars! Hence, some interior operations and phenomena can come
> from nature or from the devil while the soul is in an excellent state
> and acceptable in the Lord's sight. You should merely take care not
> to believe too readily, especially in the case of locutions, and when
> you receive them you should submit them to the judgment of the one
> who directs you. This you should do even when they seem to you to
> be certain and thoroughly reliable. Remember, son, that the firm

and substantial inclination or internal consent to such locutions can come from the very propensity or fondness we have for believing what we consider to be revealed. Hence it is well to receive such locutions with great caution and with humble and constant indifference.

Padre Benedetto's letters to his disciple throw fresh light for us on Padre Pio's mystical experiences and gifts. Padre Pio sometimes wrote with difficulty, reluctant to commit such things to writing. He said as little as possible about them and it was only his spirit of obedience which led him to mention them at all. Padre Benedetto's replies enlighten us more fully as to Padre Pio's spiritual state and bring the mystical phenomena into focus, as it were, when Padre Pio's own account has perhaps left us with only a blurred image. To Padre Pio himself these letters brought comfort and confidence by the clarity and certainty which characterised them. This was the case, for example, when he received a reply from Padre Benedetto in September 1910:

> I see clearly that he has chosen to keep you close to himself, although there is no merit on your part. By this time you can be quite sure that he intends to take full possession of your heart which he desires transfixed by suffering and love like his own. Your illness, his endearments, the holy flames, the temptations, aridity and so forth are expressions of his unspeakable love. When the Evil One tries to persuade you that you are the victim of his assaults and are abandoned by God, do not heed him, for he is trying to deceive you ... Meanwhile, the only advice I can offer you is not to do anything other than what the Holy Spirit wants to accomplish in you. Abandon yourself to his transports and have no fear. He is so wise and gentle and discerning that he does nothing but what is good. Especially when interior delights are accompanied by a deep and tender humility, they must not give rise to any suspicion and the heart must be opened to receive them.

On 3 October of the same year Padre Benedetto continued with his enlightening counsel:

> Do you want to know what Jesus is asking from you? The answer is an easy one. He wants to stir you up, shake, thresh and examine you like grain, so that your spirit may reach that cleanliness and purity he desires. Could linen keep itself perfectly clean in the cup-

board in which it is placed if it were not first made quite spotless?
Can grain be placed in the store-room if it is not free from all cockle
and chaff? So it is with the chosen soul. I am aware that temptations seem to tarnish rather than cleanse the soul, but as St Francis
de Sales says, they are like soap which when spread on the linen
seems to soil it while in reality it cleanses. All the same, you do well
to wish that the Lord may set you free from these temptations and
I myself will pray for this intention. At all costs, though, you must
not fear that the Lord will leave you in the enemy's power. He will
give the latter just as much power to torment you as serves his
fatherly plan for the sanctification of your soul. So be strong and
cheerful in spirit.

When Padre Pio was confused and troubled by conflict-
ing forces in his soul, Padre Benedetto at once came to the
rescue and explained this apparent contradiction:

You don't understand how one can have a firm and resolute will to
love God and not to offend him while at the same time feeling quite
weak and prone to evil. But nothing is so easy to explain as this
contradiction. We have opposing forces within us: the soul informed
by faith is opposed to the flesh with its natural promptings and best-
ial instincts; divine grace is opposed to diabolical instigation. As these
two opposing forces are present within us, we experience the phenomenon to which you refer. The spirit allied with grace is fighting
against the flesh allied with the devil and although the spirit main-
tains its supremacy it feels the adversary's molestations and insults.

Padre Benedetto's writings reveal his competence to guide
persons who had reached a high state of prayer. He sometimes
sent Padre Pio a copy of letters he had written to others
when he felt they suited the young friar's case. The following, dated 8 December 1912, is typical:

When the soul enjoys the Supreme Good and remains in deep and
prayerful recollection, the prayer is good and is called the *prayer of
quiet*. In this state the soul is not subject to illusions and deceptions
as in the case of visions, etc., in which the senses are involved, because
here all is spiritual. Hence we should not resist grace, but second it
by allowing it to act peacefully. The person favoured by this gift
should endeavour to understand and hear what God wants, without
thinking about what is happening within him. He should merely
recommend himself and others to the divine mercy by short prayers.

In this state of soul what should interest him is whether, when this recollection ends, he feels his heart replenished with charity and his intellectual and physical faculties refreshed, because this is a sure sign that it is God who is acting in him. It is well to prepare for this prayer humbly and tranquilly. If one is sometimes taken by surprise and plunged into recollection this is all to the good and there is then a greater certainty that it is God who is acting in the soul. Time spent in such prayer is not time wasted, for according to what has been said it is not a question of being stupefied, but of a tranquil activity in the faculties which have been seized by God. Although this action is very gentle it is none the less active.

In replying to Padre Pio's accounts of extraordinary spiritual trials and attacks of the devil, his words were completely reassuring and he spoke as a master completely sure of his ground. In 1913 he told Padre Pio:

> The things which take place within you are of such a nature as to leave no room for doubt regarding their origin. Be at peace, then, in the knowledge that it is the Lord who is acting in you. Satan's action is now quite distinct from the action of grace and by this time you must be able to discern the difference. The one who perturbs and torments you is Satan, the One who enlightens and consoles you is God.

Padre Pio was not spared the trial which St John of the Cross calls "the dark night of the soul". Evidence of this excruciating trial is present in his letters over a period of many years and, in fact, until his correspondence ceased in 1922. Those of his confrères who were closest to him in later years express the opinion that his soul was plunged in this "dark night" for the remainder of his life, even though he wrote nothing on the subject after 1922. In the earlier years of this trial, Padre Benedetto provided sure and enlightened guidance. On 9 March 1916 he wrote:

> The night in which you are immersed and which bewilders you is a most painful trial, but it is very lovable because of the fruit it produces in your soul. It is intended to extinguish human understanding so that divine understanding may take over, so that stripped of the common way of thinking and the ordinary use of the mental faculties you may ascend to what is purely supernatural and heavenly. Not only may you hope that God will return to your soul . . .

he is already working within you with an activity and effectiveness
commensurate with his intense love for you.

During the summer of 1918, while Padre Pio was enduring
extreme spiritual torment, darkness and utter desolation,
which emerges in the anguished tones of his letters, his director was at hand to accompany him step by step through this
sublime mystical experience. Padre Benedetto expressed no
surprise at what was taking place in the soul of his disciple
and his counsel was always wise and adequate. He replied
ably to Padre Pio's accounts of the "divine touch" he experienced during this period and to his later account of transverberation and stigmatisation.

Not many months were to elapse before a series of painful
events culminated in the complete separation of the two
friars. Sensational newspaper reports had drawn great crowds
to San Giovanni Rotondo. Though most visitors were devout
and animated by sincere faith, there were also acts of fanaticism on the part of those who were drawn to Padre Pio's
friary by mere curiosity. The Holy See was obliged to intervene repeatedly and to restrict more and more Padre Pio's
activity among the people. All this will be dealt with in
greater detail in a later chapter, but what is of interest at
this point is the fact that the authorities considered it advis-
able that Padre Pio should have another spiritual director in
place of Padre Benedetto of San Marco in Lamis, with whom
he was "to cease all communication even by letter". This
order from the Holy See is humanly explicable, but it was
undoubtedly a cruel blow to these two great souls who were
thus separated for the rest of their lives.

This was part of God's plan for Padre Pio and it bears out'
the teaching of many spiritual writers. To mention only one
of these, Father Jean-Pierre de Caussade in his classic treatise
Self-abandonment to Divine Providence points out that some
souls whom God leads by this path have less need of spiritual
guidance than others. By disposition of divine providence,
de Caussade tells us, death or some other circumstance sometimes takes away the guide who had introduced them into
this state. These souls are always ready to accept direction
but they peacefully await the moment at which God will

grant it to them. If such help no longer comes their way, they continue to follow the maxims given by their former counsellors.[3] Several people have reported that in later years, when Padre Pio had given them particularly wise advice and they remarked on his wisdom, he would tell them: "I received my training from Padre Benedetto."

Padre Benedetto's mortal remains were translated in March 1975 from San Severo to the cemetery in San Giovanni Rotondo. The Capuchin friars desired this, so as to bring close to Padre Pio on this earth the remains of the friar who had been his enlightened guide along the path of holiness. Padre Benedetto had always taught and written that the mystical transformation of souls takes place in the midst of trials and desolation. During the last twenty years of his life he himself had much to suffer, but never a word of complaint passed his lips. He died a saintly death in San Severo in July 1942. After Vespers had been sung on the 18th, he felt ill and retired to bed, convinced that he would soon be in paradise. He grew worse from hour to hour and died three days later. Padre Aurelio of Sant'Elia, Guardian of the friary in which he died, remained by his side and towards the end asked him if he would like them to send for Padre Pio, whom he had not seen for twenty years. To this he replied: "No, there is no need to send for him. He is here beside me."[4]

SEVEN

A Model Friar

Padre Pio has received wide publicity throughout the world by reason of the extraordinary aspects of his long life: bleeding stigmata, bilocation, ability to discern the exact state of conscience of those who sought his counsel even for the first time. However, if it is God's will to propose him to the world as a model of Christian life, it will not be for these exceptional charisms which in themselves do not prove a man's virtue. Rather will it be for his perfect observance of the Capuchin rule, for the high degree of virtue he showed at all stages of his religious life, his unequalled charity towards his confrères, his outstanding spirit of humility, his prompt obedience to authority at all levels.

Francesco Forgione entered religion a full sixty years before the Second Vatican Council opened its doors, but it is interesting to observe how fully his life corresponded to what the council Fathers laid down in the *Decree on the Renewal of Religious Life (Perfectae Caritatis)*. During these post-conciliar years most religious congregations have endeavoured to apply this decree to their community life. In most cases the emphasis has been placed on *aggiornamento* and efforts have been made to update the pattern of religious life by introducing what are sometimes drastic changes. An attentive reading of the decree itself shows how carefully its authors seek to safeguard the fundamental values of religious life. Before speaking of "appropriate changes and renewal" they point out that "all those who are called by God to the practice of the evangelical counsels . . . bind themselves to the Lord in a special way" *(P.C. 1)* and that "since the final norm of religious life is the following of Christ as it is put before us in the Gospel" *(2)*, religious "should follow him, regarding this as the one thing necessary" and "be solicitous for all that is his" *(3)*.

Nobody can deny that Padre Pio regarded this as "the one

thing necessary"; his solicitude "for all that is his" was so thorough that it led him quite soon to deep union with Christ and to a spiritual state which places him on a par with the greatest mystics the Church has known. His vocation was evident while he was still very young, when he distinguished himself among his companions by attendance at daily Mass and his devout demeanour as a Mass server. Admitted to the Capuchin novitiate at fifteen, he soon became an exemplary novice. His superiors and companions are unanimous in testifying to his holy life at this stage, although there were no external signs to presage the remarkable future in store for him. Endless examples might be quoted to illustrate his exact observance of his rule during novitiate and student days.

The conciliar decree already quoted attaches great importance to obedience, which is the acid test of a good religious. "Moved by the Holy Spirit, they (religious) subject themselves in faith to those who hold God's place, their superiors" *(P.C. 14)*. All those who lived in community with Padre Pio express their admiration for his constant and exemplary obedience which was sometimes tried to an extreme degree. Padre Pellegrino, who lived close to him during the last decade of his life and assisted him in his final hours, has many anecdotes to relate in this regard. He points out that obedience was not easy for one of Padre Pio's temperament, to one so strong-willed and of such keen intelligence. His conception of obedience was profound and completely supernatural. "The more useless the order I receive, the more willingly I obey", he confided to Padre Pellegrino on one occasion.

His letters to his superiors during the period of enforced absence from his community bear eloquent witness to his spirit of obedience. "I am acting out of pure obedience to you, for the good God has shown me clearly that this is the only thing acceptable to him and the one hope of salvation for me . . . Obedience is everything to me . . . God forbid that I should deliberately disobey even to the slightest degree the one who has been appointed to judge my exterior and interior acts" (26-8-1916). During his whole life Padre Pio did everything under the banner of obedience. Misunderstandings arose and he sometimes received a sharp letter of rebuke. Although he was distressed by what was undeserved reproof, his spirit of obedience never wavered and his immediate reply to his superior revealed unconditional and humble submission.

A striking example of the heroic degree to which he practised this virtue has come to us from the pen of Dr Giorgio Festa.[1] The event to which this doctor refers took place in 1925 when he returned to San Giovanni Rotondo for a friendly visit. On this occasion Padre Pio told him that he had been suffering from severe abdominal pains for some time and asked the doctor to examine him. Dr Festa discovered a serious inguinal hernia on the right side and told Padre Pio that an operation was necessary. The patient agreed, but as he was not allowed to leave the friary it was decided to equip a room there, while the doctor sent at once to Rome for everything required for the operation, which took place on 5 October 1925. It was only when he entered the improvised operating theatre that Padre Pio told the doctors they were to use no anaesthetic, while he assured them that he would remain perfectly still under their instruments.

It must be remembered that the Holy Office, for prudential reasons, had placed him under obedience not to allow anyone to see the stigmata, while he himself was aware how anxious Dr Festa was to see them again after a lapse of five years. Padre Pio had continued to obey this injunction to the letter, and in the present circumstances, rather than disregard an order from Rome, he preferred to endure agonising pain for more than an hour on the operating table. As the ordeal continued he uttered no complaint, but was heard to murmur: "O Jesus, forgive me if I don't know how to suffer as I ought." Just as the doctors ended their work, he lapsed into unconsciousness and Dr Festa was unable to resist the temptation to look at the five wounds. He reports that he found them just as they were five years before, although this time the heart wound appeared quite fresh. On this occasion Padre Pio had practised obedience at the cost of atrocious suffering.

His observance of poverty was no less remarkable. While

living outside his community he was most attentive to his vow and his superiors had to question him continually to discover his material needs. When his doctors prescribed expensive injections he wanted to do without them. In March 1916 he wrote to his superior:

> You already know that according to the doctor's prescription I have to have an injection every day. I want you to know that if these injections are to be continued they will prove very expensive. My heart bleeds to have so much money spent on me by our poor communities. Would it not be lawful to do without these things? Is a poor man to be blamed when for lack of means, obliged by his poverty, he refuses such treatment? And if this is lawful, why should it not be lawful for me when, after all, I am by chosen profession poorer than anyone who is poor by necessity?

In later life when his fame as a director of souls was drawing immense crowds to his friary, when money and gifts poured in for his charitable works, he showed utter detachment from such things. A poor old woman who wanted to donate something and had nothing but a box of matches, pressed this into Padre Pio's hands. He was more profuse in his thanks for this gift than for a substantial cheque received the same day from a rich benefactor. When the project for the large hospital near the friary was on the way to realisation, Pope Pius XII dispensed Padre Pio from his vow of poverty so that he might receive and manage the funds which were flowing in from all parts. In the late fifties, when the hospital opened its doors, it would have been lawful for him to live there, availing of the papal dispensation. But while he followed carefully the work and development of the hospital, he continued to live in strictest poverty in his austere Capuchin friary close by.

In 1922, seeing how he suffered from the heat, which can sometimes be oppressive even in San Giovanni Rotondo at nearly 2000 feet above sea level, a man who had benefited by his spiritual counsel sent an air conditioner to be installed in his cell. The Superior got the workmen going on it at once, while Padre Pio was busy elsewhere. When he returned to his cell and discovered what they were doing he begged them not to go on. "What will our Seraphic Father say?" he groaned.

To him that air conditioner was an offence against the poverty so greatly esteemed by St Francis.

He held the vow of chastity in such high esteem that as well as being strictly observant himself in this respect, he frequently recommended this vow to people who were seeking perfection in the world. A number of men and women still living in San Giovanni Rotondo pronounced the vow of chastity under his direction and continue to observe it.

His spirit of mortification distinguished him even as a student. All those who lived with him in the friary at San Giovanni Rotondo where he spent the greater part of his life can testify to the manner in which he mortified his body at all times. The bleeding stigmata were a source of continual and often excruciating pain, but he hungered for further suffering. When Dr Festa first examined him in 1919 he also reported on his way of life:

> He takes very little nourishment. A small plate of green vegetables between 1 p.m. and 2 p.m. and three or four sardines at suppertime are usually all the food he takes. Even then, his stomach often refuses to retain what he has eaten. He drinks neither milk nor wine, but just a little weak coffee. When possible he willingly takes a small drink of beer along with his meal. Although his physical strength is greatly reduced on this account, the same cannot be said of his spiritual energy and strength of will, which are just wonderful. He is capable of devoting long hours to confessions and conversations with his visitors and, as he told me himself on several occasions, he hears confessions for eighteen hours at a time.[2]

A great deal of light is thrown on Padre Pio's life in community by a friar from another province of his order, Padre Giovanni of Baggio, who made his acquaintance in 1934 when Padre Pio was nearly fifty years of age. Padre Giovanni had followed higher studies in Tuscany and at the Gregorian University in Rome. He served for seven years as a military chaplain and preached for many years in various parts of Italy. A man of deep piety, fully committed to the quest for evangelical perfection in the footsteps of St Francis of Assisi, he was sought by many as a spiritual guide. Such a priest could not fail to appreciate Padre Pio's spiritual worth. Padre Giovanni had longed to meet Padre Pio and when this finally became possible a relationship of sincere friendship sprang up between them, based on mutual esteem and deep spiritual understanding.

Over a period of about fourteen years Padre Giovanni visited San Giovanni Rotondo a number of times,whenever his preaching commitments took him to that region. He wrote a small book, entitled *Padre Pio Seen From Within,*[3] in which he gives an account of his private conversations with Padre Pio. From their very first meeting he found in Padre Pio a great-hearted brother who opened wide his arms to him and laid bare his soul. Padre Pio called this friar his "dear little John" and used to joke with him and tease him, while he enjoyed being teased in return. To Padre Giovanni he revealed the sorrows and joys of his heart and several times he made his confession to him, although Padre Giovanni was only an occasional visitor. The Tuscan friar gives us a revealing pen-picture:

> Padre Pio had the ingenuous candour of a little child, and he opened his heart with unspeakable affection to those who approached him in a frank and sincere spirit. On the other hand, he was relentless in dealing with any one who was shamming, who showed craftiness in his presence or did not act with a pure intention. Any slyness or duplicity was immediately evident to him and no one of this kind was well received by him, just as he rid himself (and in no uncertain terms) of visitors in search of a religious thrill or those who came from mere curiosity.[4]

Padre Giovanni also gives us a pen-picture of Padre Pio's appearance in his fifties:

> Padre Pio's wealth was completely interior, as is the case of all privileged souls who have received special charisms and an extra-ordinary mission from God. He certainly possessed uncommon human qualities. His fine well-marked features, his large bright eyes which looked into the depths of the soul, his melodious voice, his sense of humour which was enhanced by his accent and the dialectal expressions he used, and above all his keen intelligence gave him a particular charm. But all these exterior qualities amount to very little when compared to the interior worth and beauty of this friar. The stigmata themselves are merely an external sign of a much greater

and higher reality within him. Padre Pio's greatness consists especially in this interior shrine.[5]

Padre Giovanni goes on to describe his affability in the midst of his community:

> After evening devotions we all went to the hall for a show prepared by the young tertiaries in honour of Father General. Padre Pio was there, humble, dignified, smiling at the entry of each young performer. At the end of the show, when Father General had left, the young people surged excitedly around Padre Pio, who continued to smile and joke with them. He is always cheerful, jovial and most affable. You would take him to be the happiest man in the world. In the depths of his soul he *is* the happiest man, but he admitted to me that he suffers terribly from constant headache, which is worsened by almost habitual insomnia and by the summer heat.[6]

In 1935, as Padre Giovanni continued on his journey after a visit to Padre Pio, his mind kept returning to him.

> Arrived at my destination, I was still thinking of the happy days spent there close to him. I recalled the stigmata, the spiritual radiance which seemed to shine out of him and overpower those around him. At the same time I thought of the defects I had noticed in him, genuflections badly made, drumming with his fingers during meditation, letting his eyes stray towards those who came into or out of the church, taking snuff. I spoke to him about this latter habit and he told me the doctor had advised it for nasal trouble . . . I thought of his outbursts which at least at the moment seemed to indicate impatience. During Vespers I had seen him yawn five times. I had noticed these defects in him during several visits to San Giovanni Rotondo. They were quite public and he didn't hide or check them. I concluded that he acted with the maximum simplicity and naturalness and this convinced me more fully of his holiness. The saints are human beings, they have their defects and weaknesses. They aren't as we somehow expect them to be. They are neither formal nor stiff, like Byzantine or Baroque statues. They are simple, straightforward and spontaneous. This is how Padre Pio appeared to me.[7]

As regards his frugal nourishment, Padre Giovanni reports: "After community prayers we went to supper, but Padre Pio remained in the church to pray. He never took breakfast or supper. Only at the midday meal did he eat anything, perhaps a fifth of the amount eaten by a normal man." This was prior to 1946. A young American friar who entered the community in the sixties and assisted him daily for the last three years of his life, had occasion to observe his virtue. One of "Brother Bill's" duties was to carry a tray to him in his cell. At that time a Milanese doctor named Milillo used to come over frequently from the hospital to the friary to see Padre Pio. On one occasion as the Brother carried away the tray of food almost untouched, Dr Milillo remarked that "a one-year-old couldn't live on what he eats". The American friar himself tells us that he never saw Padre Pio finish any food brought to him. "He would take a forkful of spaghetti, a taste of something else, a sip of coffee and no more."

In November 1946 Padre Giovanni of Baggio visited him again.

> I was to see him in the evening, but he felt so bad that he couldn't receive anyone. Next day at lunch he was as jovial as ever. Later that day I went to his cell. He opened the door but went back to bed at once, as he had pains in his whole body. He said to me: "For some time when I lie down on the bed I feel that my body receives a certain satisfaction. I hope I am not giving in too much to nature." I admired the delicacy of his virtue: he would therefore like to keep his body stretched out on the cross all the time and never allow it any relief. I said to him: "Stay there in bed, don't come down for the sermon" (I was preaching the community retreat). But he answered: "Pray that I may be able to follow this holy retreat", and he arrived down for the sermon. That evening he came to me for confession and I felt thoroughly ashamed in face of his delicacy of conscience.[8]

Padre Eusebio Notte, who sometimes acted as his confessor during his last years, tells us that Padre Pio made a fourth vow by which he bound himself never to refuse anything God asked of him. The crucifix in the gallery of the old church, before which he was kneeling on 20 September 1918 when he received the bleeding stigmata, has four nails instead of the customary three. Some devout Capuchins point this out as a symbol of the four vows by which their stigmatised confrère nailed himself to the cross of his Lord and Saviour.

EIGHT

A Unique Confessor

When Padre Pio celebrated his golden jubilee of ordination to the priesthood on 10 August 1960, the Bishop of Foggia, Most Reverend Mgr Paolo Carta (now Archbishop of Sassari, Sardinia) wrote:

Many people look on Padre Pio as a powerful intermediary with the Lord to obtain ordinary and extraordinary graces. I am not interested in this aspect of Padre Pio and as I am insufficiently informed on the subject I am not in a position to pronounce judgment on it. What I *can* say is that Padre Pio is a great dispenser not of graces with a small *g* but of Grace with a Capital *G*. He distributes sanctifying grace to countless souls through the sacrament of confession. This is what is wonderful about San Giovanni Rotondo. The lapsed, the bewildered, those who have gone astray, the godless, regain God's grace through the ministry of this humble son of St Francis. For fifty years this abundant distribution of divine grace has continued. Never a day's respite or rest, never a day spent elsewhere than in San Giovanni Rotondo. The man who created a hospital for the relief of other people's sufferings has never allowed himself any relief from the suffering imposed on him by his priesthood and has remained at the disposal of the faithful from all parts of the world. He has been continually besieged, weighed down, overwhelmed by men and women, lay people and religious, Italians and foreigners, by important people in the ecclesiastical, civilian, political, military, artistic and scientific fields, by people of all classes who have drawn from the fountain which springs forth on the slopes of Mount Gargano.[1]

To those fifty years referred to by Bishop Carta a further eight were added, similarly devoted to the ministry of the confessional practised to a heroic degree. Padre Pio frequently heard confessions for fifteen hours a day, sometimes even for nineteen hours. He was a martyr to this duty, a martyr to the sacrament of mercy. He once said to another priest: "What a dreadful thing it is to sit in the tribunal of confession, where

we dispense the Blood of Christ! Take care not to throw it
away too easily." Because of this great sense of responsibility
he sometimes refused people absolution. To those who remonstrated with him on this account he replied: "If you
only knew what it costs me to refuse absolution! Remember
that it is better to be reprimanded by a man in this world
than by God in the next!"

Although the greater part of his time was devoted to this
ministry of the confessional and the spiritual guidance of
those who came to his friary, vast numbers of people had
recourse to him by correspondence. The former Bishop of
Foggia, already quoted, writes:

> As regards the letters he received, I learned with surprise while I
> was Bishop of Foggia that this correspondence was continually on
> the increase. In the two months May-June 1960 it was calculated that
> about 50,000 letters arrived from Italy and 24,000 from other
> countries. They contained petitions for temporal and spiritual
> favours, requests for his prayers, expressions of thanks for favours
> received. Several friars dealt with the work of answering these letters
> and kept Padre Pio informed of the requests, according to their
> importance.[2]

Mary Pyle,[3] affectionately remembered today in San
Giovanni Rotondo as "Maria l'americana", who was an
accomplished linguist, spent a great deal of her time for
several decades in answering Padre Pio's foreign correspondence.

Padre Pio was already sought as an enlightened confessor
before he was thirty. He had spent more than six years in his
home town in a precarious state of health and even then, as a
newly-ordained priest, he yearned for the ministry of the
confessional. He wrote several times to his Provincial asking
for faculties to hear confessions at least during Holy Week
and Easter, when the local priests were in great need of help.
But the Provincial did not see his way to granting this request
as he considered the hours spent in the confessional would
be detrimental to the young friar's already weak health. This
was in 1911. A year later Padre Pio renewed his plea and this
time Padre Benedetto, on 4 March 1912, justified his refusal
by saying: "Can I suppose you have a sufficient knowledge of

moral theology when you have not made a systematic study of it under a competent teacher and when, in addition, you have for a long time been unable to read it over again?" Padre Pio's sight was failing at this time and he had received a dispensation to say the Mass of Our Lady every day, while for him the obligation of the Divine Office was commuted to recitation of the Rosary. After a further year Padre Pio appealed to Padre Agostino to obtain for him from the Provincial the faculties to hear confessions and on this occasion he wrote: "I cannot suffocate this mysterious voice within me." This time, although the Provincial still refused the permission both for health reasons and because he considered Padre Pio insufficiently grounded in moral theology, he promised to grant the faculties if the young friar succeeded in passing an examination at the diocesan headquarters in Benevento. Padre Agostino suggested that another Capuchin be sent to Pietrelcina to examine him in moral theology and in a letter to Padre Pio he added: "If Jesus were to give the Provincial a sure sign of your infused knowledge (and nothing is impossible with God!) the matter would be settled." Obviously Padre Agostino was already convinced that the ailing young friar possessed infused knowledge, although at that time he was only twenty-six.

After 1913 there is no further reference in his letters to faculties to hear confessions, but presumably his request was granted not long afterwards. During 1914 and 1915, while he continued to give an account of his spiritual state to Padre Benedetto, his Provincial and spiritual director, his correspondence with Padre Agostino became more frequent. The latter, busily engaged in pastoral activity, wrote to Padre Pio from various friaries and began to have recourse to the young friar more and more frequently for advice as regards the spiritual guidance of souls in his care. Padre Pio, himself immersed more and more deeply in spiritual trials, attacked by Satan, plunged in desolation of soul, unable to understand his own spiritual state and clinging to obedience for guidance in all that concerned his soul, displayed astonishing gifts of discernment where other people's problems were concerned, as his replies to Padre Agostino clearly show. He obviously received divine enlightenment on the cases submitted to him by his former professor of theology.

A curious phenomenon, not unique but certainly rare in the history of Christian spirituality, began to emerge from the *Letters* during the spring of 1913. Padre Pio showed himself utterly submissive to the authority and teaching of his spiritual guides, yet had acquired such prestige in their eyes as to become, in his turn, their guide and teacher. Although they cannot be said to have chosen him in any formal sense as their director, it is an undeniable fact that they began to turn to him more and more frequently and to follow his advice. They seem to have come to the conclusion that his counsel was not just the fruit of ordinary knowledge or experience but sprang from a higher source of light. All this came about by degrees. Padre Pio, in his late twenties at the time, was placed in a difficult position from the psychological point of view. He was dealing with two priests who enjoyed great prestige in the ecclesiastical environment of the whole region: Padre Benedetto, who exercised the authority of Provincial Minister and Padre Agostino who was held in undisputed esteem as a professor. They were both much more learned than he, a sickly young friar who had been unable to follow more than the bare minimum of studies required for the priesthood. Moreover, Padre Agostino was seven years older and Padre Benedetto fifteen years older than the disciple to whom they now turned for guidance! Initially it cost Padre Pio a great struggle to accept this reversal of roles. When he felt urged to do so, however, he never failed to send them words of advice and encouragement and even of reproof. Later, at their explicit request, he agreed to be their guide, but this he did with reluctance and reverential fear. He considered it absurd that the disciple should become the teacher of those whose duty it was to instruct him, that the patient should write prescriptions and administer medicine to his doctor. We find him writing to Padre Benedetto on 23 July 1917:

> I have read and re-read with attention what you say on the subject of your interior sufferings and I feel a keen sense of humiliation at

being obliged to decide with regard to you, my father, my guide, my superior. I should have liked to free myself from this obligation but I cannot . . . So let us exchange roles for the moment and I will speak with all frankness and sincerity. Called upon to pronounce judgment on what you have told me, I declare before God and my own conscience that it is entirely the effect of temptation.

It would be easy to expand on the subject here by quoting from many of his letters over the next four years when his guidance of these two older men, his superiors, became more and more confident and able. I can only refer the reader to the volume of letters to which frequent reference has already been made.[4] Some of the more meaningful letters in the present context are: on vainglory (2-8-1913), on simplicity (10-7-1915), on love of God and neighbour (2-4-1919). The power and efficacy of his teaching undoubtedly sprang from his close union with God. He was frequently quite demanding and even severe in directing these older friars in the ways of the spirit, but the language in which he clothed his directives showed his sincere and genuine humility and made it quite clear that in everything else he was ready to obey them at once as his superiors.

His return to community life on 17 February 1916 was determined indirectly by the spiritual needs of a devout lady in Foggia, Raffaelina Cerase, whom he had been counselling by correspondence for almost two years, although he had never met her.[5] When she became seriously ill early in 1916 his superiors decided to transfer him to Foggia so that he might assist her. For over a month he went each day to visit her and the deep spiritual relationship which already existed between himself and this really holy soul grew deeper. They had long spiritual conversations and he sometimes said Mass in the private chapel in her home. Raffaelina Cerase died on 25 March 1916, assisted by Padre Pio to the last.

With the exception of a short absence, he remained in St Anne's Friary in Foggia until 4 September of that year, on which date he arrived in San Giovanni Rotondo where he was to spend the rest of his long life. Even in the few weeks he spent in Foggia, the emaciated young Capuchin attracted the attention of a number of devout people who attended

the Capuchin church there and he was at once in great demand
as a confessor. The oppressive heat that summer in Foggia
was very detrimental to his health and in July he was sent to
the mountain friary of San Giovanni Rotondo for a respite.
Back in Foggia in August he was once more overwhelmed
by this fatiguing ministry and in September was again sent
up to San Giovanni on the airy slopes of Mount Gargano.
This time it proved to be his final destination and for the
next fifty-two years it was to form the backdrop to the
drama of his extraordinary ministry.

*   *   *   *   *

One of Padre Pio's great merits is that of having aroused
the sense of sin in a generation from which it is rapidly dis-
appearing. This was because he himself had a profound sense
of the enormity of sin. He described himself more than once
as "the biggest sinner in the world" and had frequent recourse
to the sacrament of pardon. Padre Agostino testifies that at
least in certain periods of his life Padre Pio went to confession
almost every day. Quite often during the last years of his
life, when he had already vested for Mass, he would ask the
Guardian, Padre Mariano, to hear his confession in the
sacristy before he went to the altar.
    It is an undisputed fact that several million people converged
on San Giovanni Rotondo with one end in view, to reach
Padre Pio's confessional. What was it that drew people from
all over Italy and from many other countries to kneel at that
confessional? What did confession to Padre Pio mean? What
was there to distinguish it from the sacrament of pardon
received elsewhere? An attempt may be made here to list
the characteristics which made it so different. In the first
place, quite a large number of his penitents were sent away
without absolution. Secondly, confession to this friar gave
people such a sense of sin that they literally trembled and
shed the bitterest tears of their lives over their sins. In most
cases the result was a radical change of ideas and of con-

science. In many souls the seed of a religious vocation was sown at the confessional. In all cases there was a leap forward in the soul's relations with God. In a word, Padre Pio demanded a confession that was also a conversion. Finally, the confessor quite often mentioned the sins committed without having heard them from the penitent! The unique atmosphere of his confessional was evident even at the very beginning of his activity as a confessor, for it was not the result of experience nor did it depend on a set of rules. As he explained to his own confessor as early as November 1921, it "came down from above".[6]

Padre Pio never wasted time with his penitents. A confession lasted two or three minutes at most. He ordinarily heard about thirty persons in less than two hours, including some who had been absent for fifty years or more. This was possible because of his charism of discernment. The one condition he required in every penitent was repentance and a firm purpose of amendment. It was this demand that led him to expel some from the box with raised voice and rough words. All of this, his kind words and his rebuffs, explains a close friend of his (a lawyer named Zitto from Palermo) came from the same great heart, for he loved all those who came to him as he loved God himself. Those who were summarily dismissed sometimes rebelled interiorly against this treatment, but they were made to understand the enormity of sin and all superficiality vanished from their spiritual attitude. They got a clear view of good and evil, of God's law, his truth and justice and goodness. They went through a kind of hell, but in almost every case they returned to Padre Pio in a different frame of mind and then received absolution. It can be said that the majority of his penitents went through this experience, even people who had been practising their religion regularly before coming to him. He often detected superficiality in these and shook them out of their easygoing state by his brusque treatment.[7]

How many confessions did Padre Pio hear? Some statistics have been attempted, based on established facts. In the beginning he used to hear confessions for fifteen to nineteen hours a day. After 1923, when limits were set to his activity, and up to the end of his life, he habitually heard for several hours each day. It has been estimated that he heard at least two million confessions. In 1971 Pope Paul asked the Superior General of the Capuchins: "What is the explanation of the worldwide resonance that attracted such crowds around Padre Pio? Was it perhaps because he was a philosopher or a great scholar?"[8] We ourselves may ask: Was he a genius, a St Augustine, a St Thomas of Aquin, or a Curé of Ars? A priest who was a constant visitor and his penitent for many years heard him say one day in 1957: "At no time in my whole life did I study at academic level." Yet constantly around him were the experts of his time in medicine, science, literature, economy, politics and the arts. They came not merely for confession but also for advice on their problems at the high level of their respective professions and all of them, even those of other races and continents, received wise and learned answers. We cannot help asking ourselves: "Who was Padre Pio and where did these learned answers come from?" It seems natural to compare him to some of the extraordinary figures in Catholic hagiography: St Catherine of Alexandria who has remained famous for her incontestable answers to the most renowned philosophers of her time, St Catherine of Siena, St Gertrude and St Teresa of Avila, who have left us great works which are the fruit of divine light rather than of personal learning. What had Padre Pio to say about his knowledge? A close friend succeeded in eliciting something from his own lips on the subject: "I know all these things and see them in the One who is in me and above me", he said. A penitent has said of him that "confession made to him was something quite unique: sooner or later he made you realise that he knew you through and through and you saw yourself better than you would in a mirror." Theologians refer to this understanding of the secrets of the heart as the charism of discernment or reading of the heart. Many saints possessed it, St Thomas Aquinas, St Philip Neri, St John of God and, near to our own times, St John Vianney, the humble Curé of Ars.[9]

Padre Pio suffered for his penitents. All that he was and all that he received from God had reference to his ministry as a confessor. His voluntary penances were for him a means of increased purification, a means towards the improvement of his own Christian and religious life. They enabled him to serve as a vehicle to carry God's mercy and grace to sinners. They helped him to see clearly God's will and to discern the state of soul of each one who had recourse to him, to read even the sluggish, confused or hardened consciences of inveterate sinners. By the long hours he spent in prayer, especially at night, he maintained constant contact and a vital colloquy with God, just as a flower unfolds and is nourished under the constant action of the sun. In those long hours he bargained with God for the salvation of his penitents and prepared himself for a fruitful meeting with them and successful combat with Satan whose attacks he endured all his life.[10]

NINE

A Severe Director

In the first encyclical letter of his pontificate,[1] immediately after the outbreak of World War II, Pope Pius XII launched a strong appeal for prayer: "Pray, Venerable Brethren, pray without ceasing, pray, above all, when you offer the divine Sacrifice of love." In the years immediately following, while the world conflict continued to spread, the pope returned to this theme of uninterrupted prayer in his addresses to different groups, priests and laity. Padre Pio, always attentive to the voice of Rome, made this appeal of the Holy Father his own and in turn exhorted all who came to him to pray earnestly for the pope's intentions and the needs of suffering humanity. Thus were born his "prayer groups" which today are scattered all over the Catholic world. They grew spontaneously from his constant exhortations to prayer: groups of people who came together in a church to pray. They were not burdened with rules, organisational schemes or new prayer formulas. Inspired by Padre Pio's words, these pious people met at least once a month, with the consent of their bishop and under the guidance of a priest. They sometimes heard Mass together and then recited the Rosary. By 1950 there were many such groups scattered over the Italian peninsula and soon they began to spring up in other countries also. In 1968, at the moment of his holy death, there were more than seven hundred of these groups totalling about 70,000 members and since that date their numbers have continued to grow.

Many members of these prayer groups, particularly their leaders, had constant recourse to Padre Pio for spiritual counsel and guidance and they soon began to be known as his spiritual children. As soon as this remarkable friar had accepted any one in such a capacity, he showed himself a most demanding director. He exhorted them to constant prayer, meditation and Christian mortification and expected them to be generous in carrying their own particular crosses. From all of them he demanded steady progress in virtue and commitment to the corporal and spiritual works of mercy. When the work so dear to his heart, the Casa Sollievo della Sofferenza, at a stone's throw from his friary, began to take shape, he made great demands on these spiritual children of his. The first doctors, engineers and professional men in various fields who enabled Padre Pio's hospital to function were all spiritual sons of the humble Capuchin friar, some of them converts from a very different way of life.

When I myself went to live in San Giovanni Rotondo in 1975 I made the acquaintance of a number of people whose lives had been completely transformed by their meeting with and subsequent guidance by Padre Pio. I must admit that some of these didn't inspire much confidence. They were obviously very devoted to Padre Pio, but their stories savoured of exaggeration and even fanaticism, so I naturally discarded these and concentrated on people who struck me as well-balanced, whose stories rang perfectly true to my rather critical ears. I interviewed some of these at greater length and prepared the account of their experiences for publication in the quarterly magazine, *The Voice of Padre Pio.* Their stories throw light on Padre Pio's exceptional personality and his uncommon ability as a spiritual guide.

An engineer named Bianchi, from Northern Italy, is a typical example. I met him not far from the friary in a little shop owned by another man from the same part of Italy. The two men were deep in conversation when I entered the shop and I soon found myself involved. I had seen Mr Bianchi quite often on the altar, serving Mass or Benediction with great devotion, but had not spoken to him before. Now he introduced himself and after a little encouragement began to tell me how he had come to settle in San Giovanni Rotondo. With great frankness he explained:

> I am one of Padre Pio's converts, not in the sense that I wasn't a baptised Catholic before I met him, but because he changed my whole life and made me a fervent Catholic. I was very fond of the other sex and lived a sinful life with one woman after another. For years I kept away from the sacraments. Then I met a woman

who attracted me more than all the others, a very good Catholic, whom I married shortly afterwards, giving up my sinful attachments. Although I accompanied my wife to Mass from time to time I never approached the sacraments. My wife was very devoted to Padre Pio and not long after our marriage I travelled with her to San Giovanni Rotondo. She went to confession to Padre Pio but I myself took care to keep out of his way. Then the war intervened and it was 1947 before we returned to Mount Gargano. On the little bus which climbed the mountain from Foggia I had a disconcerting experience. Another passenger told us the dramatic story of how his little boy had been cured by Padre Pio of total deafness. The man was now taking the boy, a teenager, for the umpteenth time to Padre Pio in thanksgiving for this favour. As he told us the story I began to feel extremely uncomfortable in my sinful state. My wife went to confession as usual, but I myself couldn't face this extraordinary friar. I made up my mind, though, to approach the sacraments when I got back to my own city and this I did on several occasions. On our next visit to San Giovanni, I felt anxious to obtain Padre Pio's help to live a better life.

I won't easily forget my first confession to him. As I told him the sort of life I had lived for years, his face contracted and he grimaced as if in great pain. In the end, when I asked him if I might become a spiritual son, he agreed, but he added a warning: "If you dare to do any of those things again . . ." and he raised his hand in a threatening gesture. As I left the sacristy after confession I felt as if I were literally walking on air, a distinct physical sensation as though a huge weight had been removed from my body, as if I were floating rather than walking.

This remark of the engineer didn't surprise me at all. I had heard others who had abandoned a sinful life through a sincere confession to Padre Pio describe the same sensation, telling me that they had "found it difficult to keep their feet on the ground". Moreover, many a "hard case" like the engineer in question had told me of the expression of great pain which appeared on Padre Pio's face while he was absolving serious sins. It was as if he saw all the hideousness of those sins and his horror at what he saw was reflected in his face.

I turned my back definitely on my sinful habits [continued the engineer] and by God's grace, with Padre Pio's help, I became a daily communicant. When my wife died a few years later I felt irresistibly drawn to San Giovanni Rotondo, so I sold my home in the north and came to live here. I had suffered for years from my spine and was wearing an orthopaedic appliance when I came here, but Padre Pio ordered me to take it off and made me do my share of the heavy manual work of which there was plenty at that stage on the building of the hospital. I obeyed him without question and worked hard for many hours a day. I have never had any further trouble with my back, except for an occasional twinge when the weather changes.[2]

Another engineer who left Rome to devote himself to work for Padre Pio in San Giovanni Rotondo told me a little about his life and admitted that he had visited Padre Pio the first time "from mere curiosity". Then he said slowly, with an air of deep conviction: "I was never the same again after my first meeting with him." This sums up the opinion of a great many of his devotees. For various reasons they came to him and they will tell you, more or less in the same words: "My whole life underwent a change" or "I was never the same again."

A pattern emerged from all the stories I heard from Padre Pio's devotees, men and women who had turned over a new leaf as a result of their contact with him. These people had not necessarily been great sinners before they met him. Some were good Catholics living what was to all appearances an edifying life in their own environment until Padre Pio brought about a kind of earthquake in their lives. The pattern of his spiritual guidance which emerged was the following. When he found a person possessed of the fundamental qualities for a holy life, he took over and goaded that person on to sanctity. It was only after a number of years that such people realised what he had done, the revolution he had effected in their spiritual life. Margherita C. is just one example to illustrate what God's grace, through Padre Pio's firm direction, achieved in people of this kind. She is a sensible, matter-of-fact person whose behaviour and conversation on the few occasions on which we met suggested to me a deep spirituality and probably an interesting story, which she told me at a later stage.

I lived in a small town in Bari province about eighty miles from here. I first heard of Padre Pio in 1948. I was nearly forty when my dear father to whom I was very attached fell ill and died. I had several brothers and sisters but I was my dad's favourite and when he was gone I was desperately unhappy. At that time we all lived together in our rural home. I withdrew from the others and nursed my grief in silence. I had very little in common with the rest of the family. They were mainly occupied with material matters, while I used to spend a lot of my time in church and in the Catholic associations of our parish. One day, seeing me so desolate, a woman whom I hardly knew spoke to me about a "holy friar" up on Mount Gargano and asked me why I didn't go there to get his help and counsel as so many others did. I thought about it for a while, then followed her advice. It was in the month of March. I won't go into details of the journey which was anything but easy. I arrived towards evening and obtained rather miserable accommodation near the friary, where I was told I could go to confession to Padre Pio the following day. Now, I was a member of several pious associations in my own town, I had been going to daily Mass and communion and considered myself quite a good Catholic. I made my brief confession to Padre Pio and then poured out my grief at the death of my father, saying how desperate I was and confident that he would help and console me. To my surprise and indignation he just closed the shutter in my face and turned to the penitent at the other side without giving me absolution. I was very angry as I left the church, thinking to myself that this was no saint and that I had been a great fool to go there at all. I was still fuming when I returned to my lodging, but the people there took me very calmly and said I must wait a few days and then go back to him. My chief feeling for several days was deep resentment towards this friar, but I was afraid to receive communion as he hadn't absolved me, so I just waited. In those days he never received anyone until at least a week had elapsed from their previous confession. As the days went by my state of mind seemed to undergo a change and my resentment vanished. On the eighth day I took my place once more at his confessional. This time he seemed quite different. I told him again about the death of my father, then he continued to question me, until I suddenly said: "The Lord took him from me." "Ah!" said Padre Pio, as if he had been waiting for just that phrase which indicated acceptance of God's will. Then he spoke to me very kindly and gave me absolution.

To cut a long story short, Margherita lingered on for several weeks in San Giovanni and returned to Padre Pio each week. As she says herself: "Something quite new seemed to have entered my life and I experienced a wonderful peace and serenity, although I had no sort of comfort in my poor lodging and had to endure many hardships, including very bad weather and the inconvenience of rising so early to get to his five o'clock Mass." When her money began to run out she wondered what she ought to do, still reluctant to leave. She mentioned the situation timidly to Padre Pio who merely said: "Work and eat!" These words puzzled her, but soon afterwards some work she could cope with came her way and bit by bit little jobs were offered to her which enabled her to eat and pay for her room. Her life became very austere from sheer necessity but her happiness seemed to increase. She continued to postpone her return home and when she was offered what was little more than a hut all to herself, but with no water or sanitation, she took it. Padre Pio continued to guide her and his counsels pointed to a considerably more austere life than she had ever led at home. When some weeks had passed, her brothers who considered she was damaging the family name and prestige by her way of living, turned up in San Giovanni and made every effort to make her return home. They even enlisted the help of a police official who had married a relative of theirs, thinking to intimidate her. When all other efforts failed they tried to persuade Padre Pio to order her back home. He replied calmly: "Very well. Take her home with you if she wants to go." But Margherita had no desire to go and after some further attempts the family abandoned their efforts to persuade her. When Margherita got to this stage of her story she said: "I was learning a great many things about the spiritual life which had never come my way previously. It was as if Padre Pio had stripped me of everything I had in order to open my eyes to the wonders of the spiritual life."

In the early fifties, when the hospital had begun to carry on a limited amount of activity, with a dispensary and a ward for fifty children, Margherita's services were requested and she began to do night duty there. Although she continued to live in her poor little hut, her salary at the embryo hospital was so small that it barely covered essential needs. She felt justified in appealing to Padre Pio on this account, but he was surprisingly harsh with her. "It's only your wretched soul I'm interested in," he said, "not your material needs. Anyway, you have never lacked anything you needed since coming here, have you?"

Margherita still worked at the hospital when it was formally opened and her living conditions improved slightly. However, she continued to live a frugal Franciscan life for many more years, up to the date of Padre Pio's death in 1968: twenty years of privileged spiritual direction. Since his death she has persevered in the same austere way of life. She now lives on a small pension in a tiny apartment not far from the friary and is to be seen daily at Mass and at his tomb in the crypt. Her concluding remarks give food for thought. "Before I came here," she said, "in all the years during which I belonged to the Catholic associations in my own parish I never really learned anything worth while about the spiritual life. I got everything from Padre Pio. He opened my eyes to a completely new spiritual dimension. His direction went right down to the roots and he didn't spare me. He stripped me of pride and self-love and he taught me what our religion is all about. I can never be sufficiently grateful to God and to him for all I have received."[3]

In the vicinity of the friary I came on many others whose experiences had been similar, even though their circumstances differed greatly from those already quoted. There was, for example, a German-speaking Swiss lady, wealthy, independent, but genuinely in search of spiritual peace. She had been attracted by Hindu mysticism and was on the point of travelling to India to explore it more fully when she heard something about Padre Pio and decided to visit him. He wasted no words, but slammed the shutter of his confessional in her face. She travelled to San Giovanni Rotondo again and again, and each time the reception was identical, until at long last, when she had delved deep into her proud and self-willed soul, he chose to take her in hand. She, too, became a spiritual daughter of his and built a house near the friary, to which she and her sister retired. They live there today in seclusion, carrying out to the best of their ability the spiritual programme he gave them. Many others abandoned comfortable homes and lucrative professions once they had discovered the "pearl of great price", for which they were ready, at Padre Pio's bidding, to relinquish all.

The greater part of Padre Pio's ministry was directed towards the crowds who came to him from elsewhere. However, he always had time for a spiritual chat with his own friars and many of these had recourse to him for confession and guidance. Padre Giovanni of Baggio, the Tuscan friar already mentioned, had many opportunities to profit by his enlightened counsel. He himself was an able preacher, Superior of a Capuchin friary in Florence and later Minister Provincial in Tuscany, yet he gladly availed of every opportunity to seek counsel from Padre Pio. During a short visit in June 1935 he asked Padre Pio to give him a brief formula for personal sanctification. "Two things are necessary," he answered at once, "a right intention and self-control."[4]

In April 1936 Padre Giovanni was back again for a visit.

I had told him I sometimes omitted meditation and pleaded my preaching commitments as an excuse. He took me by the arm, then pushed me away, saying: "If that's how things are, just go away. I don't intend to pray for you any more." This rather frightened me, but he became kinder when I made it clear to him that it had not always been my own fault. The following Sunday they asked me to preach. It was Good Shepherd Sunday and I preached with a full heart, bringing in many things he had said to me about the goodness of Jesus. While I was taking off the vestments in the sacristy he passed by and said with a smile: "You're pleased with yourself, aren't you?" Perhaps he was right in this.[5]

On another occasion when I asked him to pray for me he answered: "I'm always praying for you, but I don't see the results . . ." Later he came to my cell and we sat down opposite each other. Suddenly he said: "You have judged a friar wrongly." "Who told you so?" I asked. "Never mind," he said, then continued: "Is it true that you thought badly of a friar?" I realised that as I had mentioned this to nobody he couldn't have heard it from others. "How do you know about it?" I queried. "Never mind," he said again, "just tell me if it's true or not." "It's true," I said, "but I had my reasons for thinking like that." Then he advised me not to judge by appearances and told me that a certain inconsistency between facts and words does not always indicate duplicity but merely fragility. "At all events," he went on, "even if there was insincerity in the case of this friar, it doesn't justify your harsh manner of dealing with him and with the other friars." I was stung by this. "What harsh manner of dealing?" I protested. "You are too bitter and sometimes harsh in correcting them," he said. "Even in reprimanding you could combine reproof with politeness and mildness." "You are right," I admitted, "but it seems to me that I try hard to be kind and courteous and then, when I see it doesn't work, I lose my temper." In a few words he preached me a fine sermon on meekness.[6]

On another occasion (November 1949) Padre Pio chatted with Padre Giovanni about the humility proper to a Capuchin friar. He never beat about the bush on such occasions. "He told me I should be more humble," writes Padre Giovanni.

"Pride oozes from every pore of your body", he said to me. I began to laugh but I had to admit that he was right. I asked him how he himself overcame pride. He reflected for a while, then said: "I don't know how the Lord has made me, but I feel I should have to try much harder to make an act of pride than an act of humility, because humility is truth and the truth is that I am nothing and all that is good in me is of God. When I see so many people coming to me with requests, I don't think about what I am able to give, but of what I am *unable* to give, so that many souls remain parched with thirst because I have not been able to give them the gift of God." Then he told me to throw my heart wide open to love and for this purpose to guard charity very carefully. "I can't stand criticism and speaking badly of one's brethren. It is true that I sometimes amuse myself by teasing them, but murmuring makes me sick. We have plenty of defects to criticise in ourselves, so why waste time criticising others?" Then he said to me: "In your speech and in your preaching you have a defect which you must correct: harshness. You put poison into your words instead of love and hence you obtain the opposite effect . . ." Then, as he rose to go: "Cheer up," he said. "You are a good fellow all the same!" After the holy hour he returned to me, indignant at the way it had been conducted. "Why not speak of God's love, of his power, his glory?" he protested. His last words before he left me were: "Rest assured, you'll become holy!"[7]

Padre Pio as confessor and spiritual guide frequently administered bitter medicine, but once the dose had been accepted he was always ready to reward the patient with something more palatable. A word of encouragement was never far from his lips.

TEN

His Charismatic Gifts

If we examine the lives of uncommonly holy people, we invariably find that God has endowed them with some of his own qualities as a demonstration of his omnipotence, of Christ's divinity and the holiness of his Church. The study of these gifts and charisms in the servants of God is certainly a most difficult task. In a letter to his spiritual director, Padre Pio told him that such things are beyond the limits of description in human language. When pressed for an account of his spiritual state and the action of God in his soul, he was most reluctant to comply with the request and only when he had received an explicit order did he write about these things, greatly embarrassed and fearful that other eyes might see what he had written in confidence to his spiritual guide. Even when he did his utmost to explain what was happening within him, he was still convinced that he had not done justice to the situation and might even have given a wrong impression. On 11 March 1915 he wrote: "At this point, Father, I prefer to keep silence, for I see clearly that what I have said and could say corresponds only very inadequately to what is taking place within me." A year earlier he had written:

> You asked me to give an account of my soul and I regret that I am unable to explain myself, because it is now a question of very lofty and secret things. Words are lacking in which to give even a feeble description of what passes between my soul and God in this state. The things which are taking place at present are so secret and private that anyone who had not himself experienced them could never, never form even a faint idea of them ... It is now God who acts directly in the depths of my soul without the ministry of either the interior or exterior senses. This is, in a word, such a sublime, secret and delightful operation that it is concealed from all human creatures.

Even well-prepared scholars are cautious when it comes to discussing spiritual experiences which depart from the ordinary. The tendency is to dismiss these things as being the fruit of imagination or even of a sick mind, especially when they are found in women. It is usual to argue in such cases that the subject may be the victim of illusion or may even be physically or psychologically unbalanced. In Padre Pio's case, none of the numerous doctors who examined him from time to time found any trace of imbalance or psychological deviation. During all the time in which he was undergoing untold suffering from the open wounds in his hands and feet and side, he was never known to act in an unbalanced or irrational manner.

The chief and most reliable source available for an insight into his charismatic gifts is the volume containing his letters to his spiritual directors. Although these letters cover a relatively limited period of his life, from January 1910 to May 1922, they are sufficient to show us at least the fundamental elements of his painful spiritual ascent which was so abundantly strewn with extraordinary phenomena. Leaving aside for the moment the question of his stigmata, which will be amply discussed in another chapter, the letters contain evidence of frequent ecstasies, suspension of the faculties, visions and revelations with reference to God and his attributes, to the Passion of Christ, to Our Lady and the angels. They also contain revelations regarding his own soul and the souls of others. They tell of divine locutions, wounds of love, familiarity with his guardian angel who consoled and instructed him and even acted as his interpreter for foreign languages!

To the mystical gifts which enriched his soul and raised him to close union with his Lord and Redeemer were added a whole series of charisms which were to equip him in a unique way for the mission which God evidently intended him to fulfil. Once his public life began in San Giovanni Rotondo, the evidence of these charisms left no room for doubt. His confrères, who held him in veneration, understood very little of the mysterious world in which he lived. As Padre Eusebio Notte, who was close to him for many years, has put it: "In Padre Pio the supernatural blended with the natural to such an extent that one could no longer distinguish where the natural ended and the supernatural took over."

The extraordinary charisms with which God endowed him were many: bilocation, levitation, prophecy, healing, the power to read men's hearts, the gift of tongues, and the fragrance which emanated from his wounds and which frequently announced his invisible presence. The ability to read men's hearts and consciences has been sufficiently illustrated in Chapter 8, as it refers almost exclusively to his ministry as a confessor. Of the remaining charisms, those which made him famous more than all the others were bilocation (the extraordinary capacity to be present simultaneously in two places), the gift of healing and his extraordinary perfume.

The gift of bilocation is not unknown in Catholic hagiography, but it is certainly one of the most surprising. St Anthony of Padua was renowned for his frequent bilocations and this charism is also recorded in the lives of several other saints, notably St Francis Xavier, St Martin de Porres, St Alphonsus Liguori and St John Bosco. The evidence is so vast as to leave no room for doubt that Padre Pio of Pietrelcina possessed this remarkable gift. After he had received the stigmata in 1918 he never left San Giovanni Rotondo, yet there is a long list of witnesses who testify to having seen him and spoken to him in places scattered all over the globe. A number of these statements have been placed on record in the archives of his friary. In many cases his presence served to counsel and comfort members of his big "spiritual family" in moments of particular need. At times he was seen by people who did not know him but who recognised him even years afterwards when they saw him in San Giovanni Rotondo. Frequently his visit resulted in a sudden and altogether unexpected cure when doctors held out no hope for the life of a patient.

In August 1962 a man named Magnani, in Padua, was repairing his car in his garage, lying in a cavity beneath it, when the car suddenly caught fire and caused very severe burns on sixty per cent of his flesh, including his face. Rushed to hospital he was judged to have little hope of survival. A very high fever set in, together with a kidney block and signs of heart failure. Two of the most illustrious physicians of Padua University were with him constantly but could do nothing further to check the course of his illness. His sister, in desperation, telegraphed to Padre Pio and implored his help. Next day the patient wakened as if from a deep sleep and told his sister he had seen a friar beside his bed, who blessed him. At once the man's condition improved and in a short time he was completely cured. Six months later he travelled to San Giovanni Rotondo, where he recognised Padre Pio as the friar who had come to him in hospital.[1]

A number of cases placed on record refer to conversion, to a total change of life in the persons favoured by his visit. In many instances Padre Pio appeared at the deathbed of one of his spiritual children. Most of his biographers quote the case of Mgr Damiani, Bishop of Salto, Uruguay, who left a written testimony regarding Padre Pio's visit during the hours which preceded this prelate's death. Frequently quoted, too, is the case of General Cadorna, who was about to commit suicide after the disastrous defeat of the Italian troops at Caporetto in 1917, when a friar suddenly appeared in his tent. He had never seen Padre Pio and only came to know him much later, when he recognised him as the priest who had saved his life. There is also the well-documented case of Padre Pio's presence for half-an-hour in July 1921, at the deathbed of Archbishop Paolo Schinosi, the prelate who had ordained him in Benevento cathedral eleven years earlier. Again, Dr Andrea Cardone, who attended Padre Pio constantly in Pietrelcina in his youth and maintained a close friendship with him until his death, left a written statement in October 1968, as follows. "I, the undersigned, Dr Andrea Cardone, declare that I had conversations with Padre Pio on two occasions in my home in Piazza SS. Annunziata 93, in Pietrelcina. The first was on 18 February 1965 at 9 a.m., the second on 23 September 1968 at 6 a.m. On both occasions Padre Pio was present in his mortal flesh and our conversation lasted several minutes."[2] Padre Pio died between 2 a.m. and 3 a.m. on 23 September and his visit "in his mortal flesh" to his former doctor took place several hours later!

A remarkable instance of bilocation combined with the sudden cure of one of his confrères is related by Padre Alberto. In July 1957, he tells us, Padre Placido of San Marco in Lamis who had been a companion of Padre Pio's during novitiate and student years, was admitted urgently to the hospital in San Severo, affected by a serious form of cirrhosis of the liver. Despite all efforts of the doctors his condition grew worse. One night he saw at his bedside Padre Pio who spoke to him and encouraged him to have patience. He then saw Padre Pio approach the window where he placed his hand on the glass and then disappeared.

Next morning Padre Placido felt better. He remembered the visit during the night and looked towards the window where, to his great surprise, he saw the imprint of a hand on the windowpane. He got out of bed to examine it more closely and recognized the imprint of Padre Pio's hand. He told the story to the nuns, the nurses and all those around him. The news soon spread in the town and friends and hospital personnel began to arrive to see the alleged handprint. The doctors were incredulous and quite indignant at the furore caused by the coming and going of so many people.

The chaplain notified the superior of the Capuchin Friary, Padre Piergiuliano, who came and reprimanded Padre Placido for spreading such a fantastic story. Padre Placido, however, refused to withdraw what he had reported and insisted that he had seen Padre Pio who placed his hand on the windowpane before leaving. Attempts were made to clean the window with a damp cloth and detergent, but the imprint always reappeared and it remained there for many days. Padre Alberto, who tells the story, was in charge at the local church of Our Lady of Grace. He hurried to the hospital to see Padre Placido, formerly his professor, anxious to see the imprint on the window. He says he didn't really believe the story and imagined that some nurse had left the imprint of her hand there. But Padre Placido told him what had occurred during the night and begged Padre Alberto to go to San Giovanni Rotondo and question Padre Pio himself.

Arrived there, Padre Alberto met the stigmatist in the friary corridor and before he could say a word Padre Pio enquired: "How is Padre Placido?" Padre Alberto reported that he was on the way to recovery and then told of the terrific excitement which reigned in San Severo. "Padre Placido says you came to see him during the night and that you left the imprint of your hand on the window. People are flocking there continually and the doctors and staff are upset by all this commotion. What truth is there in the story? Is it a dream or imagination on the part of Padre Placido, or did you really go there?" Padre Pio answered him: "And you, do you doubt it?" When Padre Alberto reported this in San Severo all became silent. Padre Placido recovered completely from his illness.[3]

On many occasions the friars of his community tried to elicit an admission from him as to his bilocation. Padre Eusebio Notte tells how he plucked up courage to question him on the subject one evening when he was alone with him in his cell. He mentioned a man in Rome who was a spiritual son and suddenly asked Padre Pio: "Padre, you know this man's house in Rome, don't you?" "Me?" said Padre Pio, "how could I know it when I haven't been away from the friary for ever so many years?" Padre Eusebio insisted: "But, Padre, this man says you went to his house and that he saw you." At this point Padre Pio could no longer evade the issue and he replied: "Ah, but that's a different matter! When these things occur (obviously alluding to bilocation) the Lord only permits the person concerned to be seen, not the surroundings." "Thus," says Padre Eusebio, "I had confirmation from his own lips and a wonderful explanation of the phenomenon."[4] It was only natural that his friars and his friends should try to induce him to speak of this charism. He once referred to it as "an extension of soul and body". On another occasion he disclosed that in bilocation one sometimes goes with both body and soul, while at other times an angel takes on one's bodily appearance. He gave another person to understand that a complete explanation of the phenomenon of bilocation was very difficult, but added that in every case "one knows where one is going and what one is doing".[5]

The gift of healing is so well and abundantly documented

that a volume could be compiled on this aspect alone of Padre Pio's activity. Not a month went by without some spectacular cure of men or women who came to beg his intercession when medical science had failed to find a remedy. No wonder the crowds continued to increase on the roads leading to San Giovanni, where the deaf got back their hearing, the blind their sight, the lame threw away their crutches and walked! In the first place, Padre Pio's own body defied the normal physiological laws. His fevers went so high that they often broke the thermometer, yet a few hours later he was up and about, performing his normal duties. The amount of food he ate was, according to his doctors, quite insufficient to keep him alive. His hours of sleep were negligible, certainly inadequate to maintain his strength and energy. Thus he may be said to have been a living miracle and while God would seem to have sustained him miraculously during all those years, there is ample evidence to show how the Lord used him as an instrument to heal the sick. Very many of those who came were convinced that if only they could reach him and touch him they would be made whole.

In 1946 a railway employee named Giuseppe Canaponi, in his thirties, was involved in a serious accident as a result of which his leg became completely rigid and he could only move a few paces with the aid of crutches. He tells how his wife insisted on taking him to Padre Pio two years after the accident. He went to confession and marvelled at Padre Pio's discernment of his state of soul. He marvelled still more when he found himself on his knees, a position he had not known for years! He rose, tucked his crutches under his arm and rejoined his wife in the church. They couldn't believe it, but it was true. As he had applied for an invalid pension, Mr Canaponi went some time afterwards to the appropriate office with all the papers relating to his disablement. The doctor examined him, then said: "According to these certificates you should never have been able to bend your knee again, but you are right and not the papers, because you are able to walk." This exceptional case was examined in an orthopaedics congress in Rome in the presence of eight hundred doctors and no explanation was found as to how a man with his bones in the position indicated could bend his knee and walk.

We could continue with accounts of cures of all descriptions, in many cases of children, for whom Padre Pio always showed particular tenderness and compassion. In 1957 a child of five, Emerio Ziaco of Civitavecchia near Rome, was afflicted with muscular dystrophy, a progressive wasting of the muscles. His legs became so weak that he could no longer stand. The pediatrician, Dr V. Bares, sent him to a specialist in Rome who confirmed the diagnosis and said there was no hope of a cure. However, Dr Bares reports how, to his immense surprise, the boy's father arrived one day to tell him that the child was cured. He had been taken to Padre Pio, after which he began to walk alone, then to run and ride a bicycle. The doctor examined the child some time later and found him completely cured.[6]

The extraordinary charism of Padre Pio's characteristic perfume is too well documented to leave any room for doubt as to its authenticity. It was sometimes coupled with bilocation, when the person visited did not actually see him but sensed his presence and was surrounded by this perfume. Sometimes an individual who approached him for the first time remarked this fragrance, while others present smelt nothing at all. On several occasions when he officiated at the altar the whole church was pervaded with this perfume of which the entire congregation became aware. In a great many cases his spiritual children many miles away suddenly smelt it, as an answer to their questions, a sign of his approval or a warning, as later events made clear to those concerned. His own friars experienced it not infrequently. When his blood-stained garments were laundered, the water gave forth a delightful perfume for which there was no natural explanation. Padre Clemente of Postiglione tells how, at the end of a brief sojourn in the Gargano friary in 1923 he went to say goodbye to Padre Pio. He embraced him in the sacristy and was enveloped by a perfume so strong that it almost stunned him. Each time he tried to draw away from Padre Pio the perfume grew stronger and drew him even closer, while Padre Pio continued to embrace him. "This experience," he writes, "lasted for about ten minutes and was altogether unforgettable."

On another occasion when the same friar spent some days in San Giovanni Rotondo and was appointed to bring holy communion to the sick, he was assailed by an intense fragrance when he came to the home of Dr Sanguinetti, whose widow lived there with another woman. Padre Clemente at once thought to himself: "These women! They use so much scent!" Then he recognised it as the characteristic perfume of Padre Pio. On his return to the friary he asked him: "Why do you make me smell your perfume?" to which Padre Pio replied: "Because I'm so fond of you."[7] Since his death in 1968 his perfume has been smelt on many occasions by his own friars and by visitors to his tomb.

Padre Pio also possessed the gift of prophecy, as innumerable devotees have testified. During World War II many people came to him in desperate need of help and consolation because of the prolonged silence of a relative in the fighting lines. In a great many cases Padre Pio consoled them and assured them that the soldier was alive and would return safely to them. At times he regretfully informed them that there would be no return. His information, the fruit of an extraordinary charism, was invariably confirmed by events. To a man from Genoa he foretold prolonged heavy bombing of that beautiful Riviera city. He told him that many of Genoa's fine buildings, including her churches, would be reduced to rubble. However, he assured the man that his own home would not be damaged, and this prediction proved quite correct.

Two years before the conclave in which Paul VI was elected, Padre Pio prophesised that he would be pope. The event is of such universal interest that it merits description in detail. A gentleman named Alberto Galletti, resident in Milan, was a frequent visitor to San Giovanni Rotondo and a devout spiritual son of Padre Pio. Towards the end of 1959 the Archbishop of Milan, Cardinal Montini, who held Padre Pio in great esteem, gave Mr Galletti a message for him in which he asked for the holy friar's particular prayers. Padre Pio at once promised fervent prayers, but told Mr Galletti to inform his archbishop that he would be elected pope. He gave the man this message very emphatically, adding: "Do you understand what you are to tell him?" When Mr Galletti assured him that he understood, Padre Pio placed his wounded hand on the man's shoulder and said: "Tell him so, because he must get ready." Mr Galletti returned to Milan and soon had an opportunity to give the archbishop Padre Pio's message. Cardinal Montini was taken by surprise and exclaimed: "Oh! . . . the strange notions of the saints!" When the Archbishop of Milan actually became pope in 1963, Mr Galletti wrote to him. The documents relating to this whole story have been placed in the records in San Giovanni Rotondo.[8]

Padre Pio also followed with interest and concern the course of political events in Italy during the last years of his life. Among his visitors were a number of Italian politicians including President Antonio Segni and Signor Aldo Moro, several times premier during those years. When Italy was enjoying a genuine economic boom in 1960-1, Padre Pio was far from optimistic. At that stage he foretold the devaluation of the lira and — according to numerous witnesses — prophesied in detail the economic crisis which was to hit Italy after his own death. He spoke clearly about the disastrous social and moral conditions which were to characterise the seventies and prophesied the steady advance of communism in Italy.[9] Some of his friars will tell you that he also said most emphatically that Italy would never become a satellite of the Soviet Union.

Evidence of his possession of the gift of tongues is by no means lacking. Since the rapid spread in recent years of the Charismatic Renewal movement, we frequently hear of this gift, particularly of the ability of many members to "pray in tongues" which neither they nor those around them understand. Be that as it may, in Padre Pio's case the gift of tongues meant that he could understand and speak and write languages he had never learned. Already in his correspondence prior to 1922 we find him reading with ease the letters written to him by Padre Agostino in French and in Greek. In a few instances he replied to the older friar in excellent French, a language he had never studied.[10] When questioned on the subject he explained that his guardian angel acted as his translator! In later years when penitents were arriving at his door from many parts of the world, some spoke to him in their own tongue and were immediately understood. A Roman reports that Padre Pio, in playful mood, once changed to the Roman dialect while speaking to him, and that he spoke this characteristic dialect perfectly. The American friar who was his frequent companion during the last three years of his life heard him say one day, with a perfect American accent: "Say, would you mind closing that window?" The young friar was startled, as he was alone with Padre Pio in his cell. The latter gave him a broad smile, then returned to his habitual recital of the Rosary.

ELEVEN

His Mass

Monsignor John Baptist Montini, later to become Pope Paul VI, remarked that to assist at Padre Pio's Mass was "as effective as a preached retreat".[1] Undoubtedly those who were privileged to assist at that altar were aware that something exceptional was taking place. Many who had come from mere curiosity received such a jolt that they immediately changed their way of life. For some this meant a return to God's grace after years of absence from the sacraments. Tepid or superficial Christians entered deeply into themselves and became really fervent. Others already good-living but in search of greater perfection, were so deeply affected by the supernatural atmosphere around that altar that they disposed of their property elsewhere and settled permanently in the shadow of this shrine where the Mass became the centre of their lives.

At the fifth station of the monumental Calvary which climbs the mountain close to Padre Pio's tomb, the renowned Italian sculptor, Francesco Messina, replaced the traditional figure of Simon of Cyrene with a lifelike representation of Padre Pio bowed down beneath the weight of Christ's cross. Many writers have referred to him as "the Cyrenean", a direct sharer of the cross of Christ, a precious collaborator in our Lord's redemptive work. Mgr Giuseppe Petralia, Bishop of Agrigento in Sicily said:

> I believe that the moments in which this priest was truly Christ's Cyrenean were those in which he celebrated Mass. Artists have attempted to interpret the meaning of Padre Pio's Mass and I feel sure that theologians will also have a lot to explore in that extraordinary Mass. I believe that Padre Pio received the grace and the burden not merely of renewing in a mystical manner the sacrifice of the cross but of living over again in his heart and in his body the tragedy of the Passion. He was made to suffer in those moments the agony of Gethsemane, the scourging in the pretorium, the crowning

99

with thorns, the mockery of the crowd, of the Sanhedrin and the Roman soldiers, the humiliation of the unjust sentence, the carrying of the cross, and the crucifixion with all its torments and humiliations. This was Padre Pio's Mass: a genuine participation, a mission of reparation.[2]

Another prelate, speaking in a town near Brindisi during a three-day course on the spirituality of Padre Pio, described his Mass as follows:

> It is impossible for any one who saw him celebrate Mass even once to forget it: the distinct pronunciation of the words, at that time in Latin, his recollection which seemed to open up an abyss between himself and his surroundings, the prolonged Offertory which appeared to do violence to heaven, the Consecration which rendered visible the bloodied immolation of Golgotha, his Communion in which he seemed "merged with Christ", his prolonged thanksgiving during which all present were held fast in silent meditation. For many people, especially priests (and I myself was among their number more than once) this sight was sufficient to produce a profound spiritual upheaval.[3]

Exiled for health reasons from his friary in 1909 before he had finished his theological studies, Fra Pio of Pietrelcina yearned with unspeakable longing for the day when he would be allowed to ascend the altar to celebrate the divine sacrifice. His earliest letters from Pietrelcina to his Provincial contain frequent references to the subject. On 22 January 1910 he wrote to Padre Benedetto:

> For a long time past I have been trying to suppress a very keen desire in my heart, but I confess that all my efforts have only served to make this desire more ardent. I therefore want to confide it to the one who can satisfy it. A number of people who, I believe, are aware of recent decisions of the Holy See, have assured me that if you were to ask for a dispensation for my ordination, explaining my present state of health, all would be obtained. If everything depends on you, Father, then do not keep me waiting any longer for this day!

At the time of writing Padre Pio was only twenty-three, while canon law required the ordinand to be twenty-four years old. After some months the desired dispensation was granted by the Holy See, and Padre Pio achieved his heart's desire on 10 August 1910. The Mass then became the focal point of his spiritual life. On 29 November, less than six months after his ordination he felt "the need to offer himself to the Lord as a victim for poor sinners and for the souls in Purgatory". During the years that followed, while he was still compelled to remain in Pietrelcina, there were days on which his physical weakness was so extreme that he was unable to say Mass. When he was called up for military service and assigned to a barracks in Naples in spite of his miserable health, his greatest torture on many occasions was his inability to say Mass.

Back in Pietrelcina where he was loved and venerated by his neighbours, his Mass in the parish church was already the object of comment. It sometimes lasted two hours, as he stopped for long periods apparently in ecstasy, so that the local people who earned their living by their work in the fields found it much too long and tried to avoid it. Complaints were made to the parish priest, Don Pannullo, who in turn informed the Capuchin Guardian. The latter told Don Pannullo to recall the celebrant mentally whenever he stopped during Mass, for he knew that out of obedience Padre Pio would at once submit. The parish priest expressed his doubts, but at length decided to follow this advice. While Padre Pio was saying Mass, he used to kneel at a distance from the altar and command him mentally to continue, an unspoken order which the young celebrant at once obeyed. The parish priest told this story when he was already very old. "Listen," he said, "I have one foot in the grave so you must accept what I have told you as true."[4]

A prelate who has already been quoted in previous chapters, Monsignor Paolo Carta, Archbishop of Sassari, gives his impression of a Mass said by Padre Pio at which he was present in 1960 while he occupied the See of Foggia.

At the altar Padre Pio was transfigured. His face was deadly pale, radiant and sometimes bathed in tears. There was an intensity in his fervour; there were painful contractions of his body; he had a seraphic aspect. Great silent sobs shook him from time to time. Everything about him told us how intensely he was living the Passion of Christ. One had the impression that time and space had been cancelled between that altar and the Hill of Calvary. The divine Victim raised up in those pierced hands brought home more vividly to the faithful the mystical union of the celebrant with the eternal High Priest, Christ Jesus . . . In the act of offering the divine Victim he offered himself as victim for the sins of men. When a lady asked him to define his relationship with his spiritual children, he answered: "In your midst I am a brother, in the confessional a judge, at the altar a victim." When another friend asked him in confidence if he suffered more intense pain during Mass, he nodded his head in assent. Yet another asked how he managed to remain standing at the altar, to which he replied: "In the same way as Jesus remained upright on the cross." The other persisted: "Then you are nailed to the cross for the whole duration of Mass?" "Yes," replied Padre Pio, "and what way do you expect me to be?" "Do you die too during Mass?" asked his companion. "Yes," said Padre Pio, "I die mystically during Holy Communion." "Is it love or pain which causes your death?" questioned the other, to which he answered: "It is love rather than pain."

He himself wrote in reference to his Mass: "Gethsemane, Calvary, the altar! Three places of which the third is the sum of the first and second. They are three different places, but one alone is the Person you find there." Padre Pio's Mass, then, meant his participation in the drama of Calvary. He experienced all over again each day the acute suffering which had wounded him in soul and body on the morning of 20 September 1918 when he received the visible stigmata . . . The stigmatised friar of Mount Gargano relived the entire Passion of the Stigmatist of Golgotha. In the Mass he was a victim, close to Jesus in his agony, a priestly victim making priestly reparation. From the moment at which his hands and feet and side were pierced by those wounds, Padre Pio's habitual posture was that of a man bowed down by an enormous weight.[5]

A further idea of what the Mass meant to Padre Pio can be gleaned from a number of the friars who assisted him before and during the rite. Padre Innocenzo of Campobasso relates:

For three years I was close to Padre Pio (1950-1953), appointed by our superiors to assist him in his whole ministry. I then realised more than ever that the celebration of holy Mass was the centre of his religion and piety. To me it was a mystery how he could spend so much time preparing for Mass. His alarm clock was always set for

2.30 or 2.40 a.m.. Sometimes, in summer, I surprised him on the verandah near his cell, completely immersed in meditation. Each morning I went to his cell to accompany him down to the sacristy. I always found him ready and waiting for me, with the beads hidden in his hands while he recited the Rosary.

Padre Alessio Parente continues:

Rosary beads in hand, pale and exhausted, invariably helped by one of his confrères, Padre Pio used to make his way to the sacristy to vest for Mass. When he was ready, with slow uncertain steps, humble and recollected, he moved with great difficulty through the dense crowd of people who were unwilling to move aside, and approached the altar to renew the passion of Jesus. As he walked he recited in a low voice the Miserere psalm with deep compunction and humility.

The Tuscan friar, Padre Giovanni of Baggio, assisted many times at Padre Pio's Mass when his preaching commitments took him to the Apulia region. Padre Giovanni describes Padre Pio's manner of reading the Epistle and Gospel, which he always read "very calmly".

He seemed to be meditating on every word, and to be carried out of himself by every action of the rite. He read with emotion, in a low and almost weary voice, unhurriedly, pronouncing every word distinctly. Certain nervous twitchings of his face, certain glances upwards, certain movements of his head as if he were chasing away something vexatious, suggested deep suffering and great efforts to keep himself from being caught up in ecstasy.[6]

Padre Alessio Parente describes various moments of this extraordinary Mass, of which the Offertory, he says, was an outstanding feature.

He remained for a long time as if unable to move, his eyes full of tears invariably fixed on the crucifix, while he offered to the heavenly Father the bread and wine that were to become the body and blood of Jesus. When he raised the paten and chalice, his sleeves fell back a little and revealed the wounds in his hands on which the eyes of all those present rested with deep emotion. But the culminating point of his Mass was the consecration. With sobs and tears, indescribably convulsed, the stigmatised friar re-enacted the divine tragedy of Calvary to the point of showing forth in his own pierced flesh the awful torment of Jesus crucified.

On some occasions, as many of his fellow-friars relate, his wounds bled so profusely at this point that additional bandages had to be brought to the altar. It was during Padre Pio's Mass that many people were shaken to the point of renouncing a sinful life or were even converted to the Catholic faith. A renowned disbeliever, Alberto Del Fante, converted to the faith through Padre Pio's intercession, remarked: "Padre Pio's Mass is different from all the other Masses celebrated throughout the world, not that the liturgy is different, not that there is a different interpretation, but because he re-enacts the Passion of the Nazarene by becoming a living sacrificial victim."

Many people remarked the transformation which seemed to take place in Padre Pio after the Consecration. His countenance appeared to change and people often said: "He seems to be Jesus himself." During the prayer for the living before the Consecration and again during the prayer for the dead, Padre Pio remained absorbed for a long time in prayer. He was praying then for his spiritual children and for the innumerable souls who had been recommended to him. As someone put it, he was "bargaining with God for souls". For sinners, for the conversion of those steeped in vice, he was ready to pay any price in personal suffering. Had he not, in fact, already in his early thirties, offered himself to God as a victim for sinners?

Another impressive moment during his Mass was that which immediately preceded his communion. Loudly and distinctly he pronounced the words: "Lord, I am not worthy", while he struck his breast with astonishing force. It was hard to imagine so much strength in his pierced hands, or that his wounded chest could stand up to such severe blows. Then he received the Body and Blood of his Saviour and remained bowed over the altar for quite a long time, seemingly completely absent from the world around him. "After his long ecstatic thanksgiving," says Padre Alessio Parente, "he purified the paten and chalice with what was almost scrupulous care. Here, too, he expressed his profound faith and ardent love for Jesus in the Blessed Sacrament." The reading of the prologue to St John's gospel, which figured towards the end of Mass before the liturgical reform introduced by Vatican II, was also marked by deep emotion on the part of Padre Pio. His face was radiant as he read this sacred text and his voice trembled at the words "and the Word was made flesh". In spite of his wounded feet, he would make a profound genuflection at this point, his knee touching the ground as he adored the Word Incarnate.

* * * * *

I myself first visited San Giovanni Rotondo in 1956 and assisted at Padre Pio's extraordinary Mass. As an Irish Catholic I was deeply devoted to the Mass at which I assisted most mornings. It was mid-winter at the time of my visit and the early morning call to climb the steep hill to the friary for 5 a.m. Mass was a penitential rite in itself. I remember clearly how disedified we visitors were by the behaviour of the local women who waited at the closed door of the church that morning, and elbowed us roughly when we tried to get near the altar. They were noisy and far from devout, but the moment Padre Pio appeared they were completely silent. I can add my voice to the chorus of those who describe his Mass as "something utterly different". Padre Pio's movements as he ascended the altar on his pierced and bleeding feet were obviously those of a man in great pain. His pallid, pain-lined face suggested the face of the suffering Christ bowed down beneath the weight of the cross. When Mass was over and, assisted by two friars, he had retired to the sacristy, we went closer to the little altar and found that beneath the carpet were several cushions which alleviated to some extent the pain in his wounded feet as he stood and moved from side to side during the sacrificial rite. That was twelve years before he died, but even then he seemed extremely feeble and could only move about with great difficulty, always assisted by some of his brethren. During the last months of his life he was dispensed from standing at the altar and he sat while celebrating Mass. At that stage he was usually brought from his cell to the church in a wheelchair. Rarely did he fail to keep his daily appointment at the altar. In fact, he said Mass on the last day of his life, before an immense throng of his spiritual children and devotees from all parts, who had come to San Giovanni Rotondo to celebrate the fiftieth anniversary of his stigmatisation. I was unable to be present at that last Mass. In view of the solemnity of the occasion, the ceremony was filmed and the film has been widely circulated in recent years throughout the Catholic world.[7] The stigmatised friar of Mount Gargano had very few hours to live as he performed the long rite of that Missa cantata, which was a final act of obedience to his Superior and a fitting farewell to his immense spiritual family.

TWELVE

The Devil's Assaults

Charles Baudelaire, nineteenth-century French poet, said that "the most cunning trick of the devil consists in persuading us that he doesn't exist. Thus we find some people sustaining that the devil is merely a negative dialectic hypothesis." Father Dominic Mondrone, SJ, quoted earlier, comments on this statement as follows:

> While it ought to be much easier to demonstrate the existence of Satan and his action in a more and more troubled world, less and less is said of the terrible adversary as time goes on. There is a sort of conspiracy of silence on the subject ... Yet the Church has constantly taught us that the devil exists and must be reckoned with in the Christian life, and her teaching is soundly based on the Gospel itself.[1]

Pope Paul VI spoke explicitly on the subject in a memorable general audience in 1972.

> What are the greatest needs of the Church today? Do not let our answer surprise you. One of the greatest needs is defence against that evil which is called the devil ... Evil is not merely a lack of something. It is an effective agent, a living, spiritual being, perverted and perverting ... We know that this dark and disturbing spirit really exists and that he still acts with treacherous cunning.[2]

Vatican II also stressed the power of the devil. In the *Constitution on the Church in the World* we read: "The whole story of man's history has been the sorry story of dour combat with the powers of evil, so our Lord tells us, from the very dawn of history until the last day"(*37*). Again: "although set by God in a state of rectitude, man, enticed by the Evil One, abused his freedom at the very start of history ... What Revelation makes known to us is confirmed by our own experience. For when man looks into his own heart he finds that he is drawn towards what is wrong and sunk in many evils which cannot come from his good Creator" (*13*). The

Decree on Missionary Activity states that "missionary activity purges of evil associations those elements of truth and grace which are found among peoples . . . It restores them to Christ their source who overthrows the rule of the devil and limits the manifold malice of evil" (*9*). Speaking of those who have not yet received the Gospel, the *Dogmatic Constitution on the Church* states that "very often, deceived by the Evil One, men have become vain in their reasonings, have exchanged the truth of God for a lie and served the world rather than the Creator" (*16*). "We put on the armour of God," says the same document, "that we may be able to stand against the wiles of the devil" (*48*).

Although most Christians today believe without difficulty in the existence of the devil, they find it hard to accept the fact that, by divine permission, many people have been physically tormented and attacked by Satan, beginning with some of the holiest men and women the Church has known. These sceptics will find it very difficult to accept accounts of such diabolical phenomena and nobody can force them to do so. Padre Pio was never possessed by the devil, but he was grievously tormented by the spirit of evil as he clearly describes in his *Letters to his Spiritual Directors.* Says Father Mondrone:

> We might wonder why God permits such things. It could be to show forth the holiness of some soul, to increase his merit and eventually to humiliate the devil who is always vanquished in the end. As far as I am concerned, until somebody proves to me that Padre Pio was a person full of complexes, an hysteric, a poor deluded creature, and that his spiritual directors were similarly deluded, I assure you that I have no difficulty in accepting these facts.[3]

Padre Pio of Pietrelcina grappled with Satan even from his early years in his own home. As a young priest he was the constant object of insidious temptations of which he speaks immediately after ordination in a letter written to Padre Benedetto on 17 August 1910. "The devil tries to make me lose my peace of soul," he wrote, "chiefly by means of temptations against holy purity which he arouses in my imagination." Two months later, on 20 October, he was to write: "Temptations pursue me more relentlessly than ever and they are a source of great suffering . . . Even during the hours of rest the devil does not cease to torment my soul in various ways", to which his holy director replied eight days later: "Temptations are the sure sign of divine favour and the fact that you fear them is the clearest proof that you do not yield to them. The more violently the enemy attacks you the more you must abandon yourself to the Lord, confident that he will never allow you to be overcome." On 29 November of the same year Padre Pio wrote once more: "Dear Father, the enemy of our salvation is so furious that he hardly leaves me a moment's peace and wages war on me in a variety of ways." And some months later: "The devil continues to make war on me and shows no sign of admitting defeat . . . Even in ascending the altar I am aware of these attacks, but Jesus is with me so what should I fear?"

During Holy Week 1911 he wrote: "Even during these holy days the enemy is making every effort to induce me to consent to his impious designs. In particular this evil spirit tries by all sorts of images to introduce into my mind impure thoughts and ideas of despair." We might quote many other letters written by Padre Pio to his director during this period, all of which testify to the constant efforts of Satan to place obstacles in the path of the holy young Capuchin and dissuade him from his generous purpose of complete self-donation for God's glory and the salvation of souls. Rather than continue to list the occasions on which he wrote to this effect, we refer the reader to Volume I of his *Letters*.

In January 1912 Padre Pio mentioned for the first time Satan's physical assaults. In a letter to Padre Agostino he wrote: "The ogre won't admit defeat. He has appeared in almost every form. He paid me a visit during the past few days along with some of his satellites, armed with clubs and iron weapons and what is worse, in their own form as devils. I can't tell you how many times he has thrown me out of bed and dragged me around the room." About this time Padre Benedetto, his Provincial, began to write less often and Padre Pio confided many things to his former professor of theology, Padre Agostino. Later in January we find him writing: "The ogre with many of his fellows does not cease to beat me, I was about to say to death. This happens every day except on Wednesdays. But *Monsieur* [he means the Lord] and the other heavenly persons make good all my losses by their frequent visits." In March of the same year he refers to the agony he endures in hands and feet and side from Thursday to Saturday, then continues: "The devil in the meantime does not cease to appear to me in horrible forms and to beat me in the most terrible manner." He describes an exceptionally violent physical attack by Satan one month later: "I was still in bed when those wretches visited me and beat me so savagely that I consider it a very great grace to have come through it alive, for it was a trial far beyond my strength." As time passed the assaults of the evil one became more and more violent. On 28 June 1912, he wrote to Padre Agostino:

> I had a very bad time the night before last. From about ten o'clock until five in the morning that wretch did nothing but beat me continually. He presented to my mind many diabolical suggestions, thoughts of despair, distrust of God . . . and I really thought that was the last night of my life, or that if I did not die I should lose my reason . . . When that wretch left me, my whole body became so cold that I trembled from head to foot, like a reed exposed to a violent wind. This lasted for a couple of hours. I spat blood.

The devil made every effort to prevent him from continuing his correspondence with his spiritual directors and when Padre Pio showed no sign of weakening, "they hurled themselves upon me, cursing me and beating me severely, while they threatened to destroy me if I did not change my mind . . . The devil threatens that if I obstinately refuse to pay attention to him, he will do things to me that the human mind could never conceive".

The young Capuchin's correspondence with his spiritual fathers seemed to enrage the powers of evil to an extraordinary extent. In November 1912 a letter from Padre Agostino, when opened, proved to be just one large blot of ink and was quite illegible. The parish priest of Pietrelcina testified to this fact and said that "when the letter had been placed on the crucifix and sprinkled with holy water it was possible to read it". This letter was dated 6 November 1912. Some time later another letter from Padre Agostino, opened by Padre Pio in the presence of the parish priest, was found to consist of a completely blank sheet of paper.

Then there were Satan's clever attempts to deceive the young friar completely. He tells how the arch enemy appeared to him in the guise of a Capuchin who brought him a strict order from his Provincial to cease all correspondence with Padre Agostino, telling him that this was an offence against poverty and a serious hindrance to perfection. Padre Pio shed bitter tears on this occasion, completely deceived by the tempter until his guardian angel revealed the deception to him.

The early months of 1913 were marked by even more violent bodily assaults on the frail and sickly body of the holy young Capuchin. He tells how the devils tried to persuade him to burn Padre Agostino's letters without reading them, and when he refused to comply, flung themselves upon him like so many hungry tigers, cursing him and threatening to make him pay dearly for this refusal. "They kept their word," he wrote, "for from that day onward they have beaten me every day." Again, in the weeks which followed, he wrote: "They vent their anger on me continually . . . my body is bruised all over from the blows I receive at their hands. More than once they went so far as to pull off my nightshirt and beat me in that state . . . they sometimes throw me out of bed." There are also references at this time to the loving treatment he receives at Jesus' hands. "At times he has even lifted me from the floor and put me back in bed", he wrote to the Provincial on 8 April.

All through this period of tremendous trial and torment at the hands of Satan and his satellites, Padre Pio expressed his firm conviction that God was making use of these torments for his purification and he mentioned continually the tender intervention of Jesus and Mary after each satanical attack. Then came a change. This type of purification would appear to have ended, as we find no mention of diabolical assaults in the following year. But his purification continued, although God had begun to use a different means to this end. Padre Pio's letters now began to tell of appalling spiritual darkness, "when such dark clouds gather in the heavens of my soul that not even a feeble ray of light can penetrate ... It is deep night in my soul, exposed to extreme torments and mortal agony". The divine goodness was represented to him in a manner which was torture to him, since he could only yearn for it from afar with extremely painful longing but was denied possession of it. He described this torment as being so severe as to be indistinguishable from the atrocious pains endured by the damned in hell.

At about this time Padre Pio had begun to direct a number of holy persons by correspondence and his letters are masterpieces of spiritual direction. All the time, however, sometimes expressed explicitly, can be seen the underlying agony of his own soul which had entered the "dark night" so graphically described by St John of the Cross. This "dark night" is the trial which God seems to reserve for those who have followed him with utter generosity and are destined to reach the highest peak of holiness.

Many commentators on the life of Padre Pio have voiced the opinion that this "dark night", this state of atrocious spiritual torment, accompanied the holy friar of Mount Gargano for the rest of his long life. As he went from strength to strength in his direction of others and his wonderful charism of discernment emerged more clearly, drawing ever greater numbers to seek his guidance, this extraordinary friar remained in complete darkness as regards the state of his own soul. Padre Agostino in particular has been able to hand on to us many precious details in this regard, as he was in more or less constant touch with Padre Pio for many years and kept a diary in which he entered particulars of what he observed in his holy confrère.

One such entry dating from 1911 is particularly worthy of mention. At that time Padre Pio had already been "exiled" from his community for more than two years, but in October 1911 his superiors ordered him to return to conventual life in the little community of Venafro. Here he remained only a very few weeks, for his health deteriorated to an alarming degree and he was obliged to return early in December to Pietrelcina. While in Venafro the young friar was favoured with frequent ecstasies which were almost invariably accompanied by diabolical apparitions, as Padre Agostino, an eyewitness, relates.

> At first the devil appeared to him in the form of an ugly black cat. Then as nude young women who danced obscene dances. The third time, without actually appearing, the devil spat in his face and the fourth time, still invisible, he created a deafening din. The fifth time he appeared as an executioner who flogged him and the sixth in the form of a crucified man. The seventh time the devil presented himself as a young man, a friend of the friar, who had visited him a short time before. The eighth time he appeared as Padre Pio's spiritual director [Padre Agostino himself], the ninth in the guise of the Provincial, the tenth as Pope Pius X. On other occasions the Evil One appeared to him as his guardian angel, as St Francis, as our Blessed Lady.[4]

Frequent reference has been made in recent years to Padre Pio's "mission". This is generally taken to mean his priestly ministry to souls on a worldwide scale. But a friar who was close to him during his last years prefers to see this "mission" as a long and dreadful battle with the enemy of men's salvation, with Satan as prefigured in the vision with which the young aspirant was favoured in 1903, a few days before his entry to the Capuchin novitiate. His life was spent in wrestling continually with Satan, snatching innumerable souls from his grasp. In 1920 Padre Agostino wrote in his diary that "from 1918 Satan was completely vanquished and the servant of God, Padre Pio, no longer experienced the slightest temptation. The devil no longer had any power over him, but he continued to launch furious attacks against the work in which Padre Pio was engaged".[5]

Satan's hatred for this extraordinary Capuchin priest was made known through the mouth of more than one possessed person who was brought to San Giovanni Rotondo. His confrères tell of several occasions on which possessed persons, shrieking and blaspheming, when brought into Padre Pio's presence became silent and calm.

Padre Alberto d'Appolito relates an episode which clearly demonstrates Padre Pio's combat with the spirit of evil.

In 1964, I was superior of the friary in San Severo, not far from San Giovanni Rotondo. One of the community, Padre Placido, was held in particular esteem by the local people for his holiness and goodness and he blessed many sufferers in body and soul with favourable results. One day they brought him a girl of eighteen from Bergamo who was possessed by an evil spirit and they asked him to exorcise her. At the sight of Padre Placido the girl became furious, struggled and yelled, cursed and swore and hurled filthy words at the Capuchin father, attempting even to attack him physically. Padre Placido was perplexed, then he advised her relatives to take her to Padre Pio. When she arrived in his presence she began to hurl invective at him, interspersed with curses. Padre Pio did not feel he had the strength to exorcise her, so he merely blessed her. A few days later a group of friars, authorised by the local bishop, attempted to carry out the exorcism, but due to the girl's mocking laughter and sneers as she derided them for their lack of preparation by "prayer and fasting", in the words of the Gospel, they were obliged to desist from their purpose. Padre Pio said nothing when he heard the news, but he became quite sad. On the following night he rose to pray and intercede with the Lord for the liberation of this unhappy creature from the power of the devil. The Evil One took his revenge and dealt him such a severe blow from behind that he fell heavily face-downward and received a deep gash on the forehead. The wound bled profusely and his cheeks swelled up. He cried out loudly as he fell and the Guardian, with Padre Eusebio, came running to his cell. They lifted him from the floor and sent at once for the doctor who disinfected and bound up the wound. In this state it was impossible for Padre Pio to say Mass. Before the church was opened next morning the faithful waited as usual in the square. Among them was the possessed girl who began to yell: "Last night I hit that old fellow . . . you'll see whether he'll come down to say Mass . . ."

Nobody attached importance to her words, but when the hour for Mass arrived the Guardian came out to tell the people who packed the church that Padre Pio was unable to say Mass. The possessed girl continued to cry out as before: "The old fellow won't come down to say Mass . . . I hit him last night."

That same morning, [continues Padre Alberto] I myself had gone to San Giovanni Rotondo to ask Padre Pio's advice, but before I reached the church I heard the comments of the people on what the possessed girl had shouted. I went along to Padre Pio's cell and found him in a pitiful state, his forehead bandaged and his face quite swollen. I asked him what had happened, to which he replied: "I fell last night." Then I said: "Father, in the square I heard them saying that the devil who has taken possession of that poor girl gave you a punch in the back and knocked you down. Is that true or is it just the people's gossip?" Padre Pio seemed perplexed. He looked at me for a few moments, then replied quietly: "Everything is possible."[6]

Mary Pyle, the American lady who lived for many years in San Giovanni Rotondo, was among the crowd that morning. She told the friars later that the possessed woman had shouted: "Pio, I've known you since you were small." She also told them that when the exorcist had asked the evil spirit: "Where were you last night?" the answer was: "I was upstairs to see the old man I hate so much, because he is a source of faith. I would have done more only the white lady stopped me." In point of fact, the friars had found Padre Pio on the floor bleeding from his wound, but with his head on a cushion. When they asked him who had put the cushion under his head he replied quite simply, "Our Lady". The cushion can be seen today in his cell, stained with the blood he shed that night when the devil attacked him so furiously.

With the exception of what he wrote under obedience to his spiritual directors during his enforced sojourn as a young priest in his own home, Padre Pio was extremely reticent on the subject of the mystical phenomena which marked his entire life and very seldom gave his confrères any inkling as to his tremendous combats with Satan. Occasionally, though, those close to him got a glimpse of these phenomena. In 1916, during the brief period which he spent in St Anne's Friary in Foggia before he was finally assigned to the community in San Giovanni Rotondo, the members of the Foggia community had tangible evidence of the devil's attacks on their holy young confrère. A number of them tell the story of one memorable day when the local bishop was visiting the friary and a diabolical din broke out in the cell occupied by Padre Pio immediately over the room in which the bishop was being entertained. The story is even ludicrous, for the sounds of combat became so terrifying that the bishop jumped to his feet and hurriedly left the friary, forgetting in his haste to take his hat which the friars had to send after him!

One evening, when Padre Pio had finished speaking to the people from the window of the old church in San Giovanni Rotondo, he looked out over the throng assembled in the square and murmured as if to himself: "If all the devils that are here were to take bodily form, they would blot out the light of the sun." As it happened, the microphone was still alive and a number of people heard this remark quite clearly. During the last years of his life, when he spent some time each day on the verandah near his cell, always in the company of one or more of his confrères, he would often stare fixedly at something the others couldn't see, and when asked what he saw, reply, "a hideous face".

In the thirty-first chapter of her autobiography, the great St Teresa of Avila described how the devil tormented her even in public, then drew a profound conclusion. "It edified me greatly," she said, "to find that when the Lord gives him permission the devil can do so much harm to a soul and body which do not belong to him. What, then, I thought, will he not do when he has them in his possession?"[7]

Padre Pio of Pietrelcina is a disconcerting figure for our times. He brings us face to face with the unpleasant reality of Satan's action in our midst, a reality which many twentieth-century Christians prefer to ignore. "A terrible reality, mysterious and frightening", says Pope Paul VI. "He still acts with treacherous cunning. He is the secret enemy that sows errors and misfortunes in human history."[8]

Times have changed, but the age-old combat between good and evil continues, and perhaps a significant part of the "mission" of the humble stigmatised Capuchin of Mount Gargano is his power to arouse in superficial Christians a salutary fear of the enemy of mankind and a desire to have recourse to sanctifying grace.

THIRTEEN

His Love for the Church

As befitted a true son of St Francis, all through his long life Padre Pio was filled with a lively "sense of the Church" to whose service he was genuinely and generously committed. In all circumstances without exception he showed deepest respect and unquestioning obedience to the Vicar of Christ, convinced, as Father Faber has put it, that "what is done to the pope is done to Christ himself".

In a first study meeting on the spirituality of Padre Pio, held in May 1972, one of the principal orators dealt amply with the theme "Padre Pio and the Church".[1] He pointed out that Padre Pio had three great loves: Christ, the Church and Our Lady, three loves so closely united that they might be considered as different aspects of one devotion. "All men are called to enter into this family of God," said Padre Bernardino, "and the individual Christian must bring his contribution to the body for the benefit of all the members. True Christians do not belong to themselves alone but must realise that they are at the service of all the others." The Second Vatican Council returned to this theme continually in many of its documents. It pointed out, in the first place, the pre-eminent place of those whom the Holy Spirit has called to govern, teach and sanctify the people of God.[2] Padre Pio entered most fully into this divine plan and made a huge contribution to the consolidation and extension of God's family. Nothing but a firm and genuine adherence to this doctrine can explain his attitude towards the Church and towards religious authority during those extremely painful years when this very authority which he loved and esteemed subjected him to what can only be described as excruciating torment. God makes use of many different instruments in leading souls to holiness. To be exposed to torment and persecution by one's declared enemies is a severe trial, but surely the most searching and agonising moral suffering ensues when our tormentors are those we love and venerate.

When we scrutinise the life of this humble Capuchin friar, when we interrogate those who were privileged to live with him at any period of his religious career, we shall never find a single instance of disobedience or the slightest lack of filial submission to those who were placed over him. His attitude towards the various popes who succeeded each other during the eight decades of his life was identical: the loving, prayerful, submissive attitude of a loyal son of the Church. During the years when he was subjected to particular trial by the Holy See itself, there were many who would have wished to intervene in his defence, aware of his complete innocence of the charges brought against him, but he himself would brook no such action. He always hastened to make it clear that we must never question the orders which come from superiors, but simply abide by them and carry them out to the best of our ability.

Although he visited Rome only once, in 1917 when his sister was about to become a Bridgettine nun, his thoughts went frequently to the home of Christ's Vicar. In the first years of his obligatory sojourn in his own home, it was to Pope St Pius X that his filial thoughts were directed. He undoubtedly loved this pope with a great love, as we learn from his letters at the time. When this great pontiff, broken-hearted at the outbreak of World War I, passed to his eternal reward, Padre Pio was deeply affected, as is obvious from a letter he wrote to Padre Agostino on 7 September 1914. He hoped and prayed that the Church might have a "worthy successor to the great Pope Pius X, whose equal Rome has never known" and he went on to speak of him as "the first, the greatest and most innocent victim of the fratricidal war" which had just broken out.

It was during the reign of Benedict XV, whom he had seen the previous year in Rome, that Padre Pio received the stigmata, and this was the first pope to take an interest in him. When the press took up the sensational news which had leaked out of the friary in 1919 and many inaccurate reports were spread about the happenings in San Giovanni Rotondo, the pope insisted on being properly informed. He sent a distinguished prelate, Mgr Benvenuto Ceretti, Titular Archbishop of Corinth and later a cardinal, to investigate, and was pleased with the report he received. He sent further emissaries to follow the course of events on Mount Gargano and in a message to the Archbishop of Manfredonia stated that "while it was well to proceed cautiously, it was not good to be so incredulous". Later, from his personal conviction of Padre Pio's genuine holiness, the same pope was to refer to him as "one of those really extraordinary men whom God sends on earth from time to time for the conversion of mankind".[3] A reliable witness, Doctor Giorgio Festa, in a book published in 1949,[4] reports several occasions on which Pope Benedict spoke out in favour of Padre Pio. In the first instance, listening to a man who had been converted a short time before as a result of a visit to Padre Pio, the pope replied: "Oh yes, Padre Pio is truly a man of God; some people have doubted this, but you will help to make him known." On another occasion, speaking to a consultor of the Holy Office, the Pope said: "I find that Padre Pio leads souls to God. As long as this is his mission, I must stand by him." In yet another conversation with a visiting priest he remarked: "Padre Pio is a really great soul."

It was during the pontificate of Pope Pius XI that Padre Pio was subjected to those extremely painful trials which in the end redounded entirely to his credit. During those years a succession of apostolic visitors arrived in San Giovanni Rotondo and at the end of these investigations, which were the cause of intense suffering to the stigmatised friar, the Holy Office declared that it found "nothing supernatural in the facts attributed to him", while the faithful were exhorted to keep away from him. This was perhaps the most painful period of Padre Pio's whole life, but it served to show beyond all shadow of doubt his profound devotion and attachment to the Church and his unshaken loyalty to Christ's Vicar on earth. Pius XI had been elected in 1922. Already in that year Padre Pio was forbidden to have any further contact with his own spiritual director, Padre Benedetto. This was a very severe blow from which he suffered deeply until the latter's death twenty years later, during all of which time the two holy friars never met again. From 1923 onwards for a full ten years the Holy Office conducted a series of investigations into the facts reported about this extraordinary friar on Mount Gargano who continued to attract the attention of the entire Catholic world. As a result, a succession of exhortations, orders and decrees gradually deprived him of almost all his priestly faculties.

While indignation and protest were rife all around him, the innocent victim of these severe measures behaved as he had always done, as a docile son of the Church who bore for the love of his crucified Lord the torrent of calumnies launched against him. The final cruel blow was the arrival of a decree from the Holy Office, dated 13 May 1931 and addressed to the Father General of the order. It was the unpleasant duty of the local Superior to communicate to Padre Pio the instructions received from Rome. He called him out of the choir and in his great embarrassment blurted out the unpleasant news without any preliminaries. By this decree Padre Pio was prohibited from saying Mass in public and from hearing the confessions either of the people or of the friars. When he received this news, Padre Pio raised his eyes to heaven and his only remark was: "May God's will be done!" The Guardian attempted to console him, but Padre Pio found no comfort except in his crucified Lord. He returned to the choir and remained there in prayer until after midnight. This painful situation lasted for a full two years, during which time Padre Pio was never heard to utter a word of complaint. He was, as he had always been, docile, humble, obedient, and patient with all. For him all this was simply God's will and there was nothing more to be said.

It is only when we consider Padre Pio's immense zeal for the salvation of souls that we can have some inkling as to the depth of suffering which this prohibition caused him. Padre Agostino, his spiritual director at that time, came to pay him a visit a few days after the decree had been made known. He wrote in his diary:

We were both deeply moved and he shed tears for a few moments. Then we talked. He told me how deeply he felt this unexpected trial and I consoled him as best I could. I told him he would have to obey to the letter. "You must remain on the cross," I said, "and men will continue to drive in the nails. All will be for God's glory and the good of souls." To this he replied: "It is precisely because of souls that I feel it so much." I told him he could continue to pray and suffer and that Jesus could save many souls even without his ministry by just accepting his sufferings."[5]

Padre Pio continued to bear trustfully and courageously what he termed his "imprisonment". For him all this was simply God's will and he was often heard to say: "The hand of the Church is gentle even when it strikes us, for it is always our mother's hand."

In 1933 Pope Pius XI ordered a careful examination of the sources from which the accusations against Padre Pio had come. He became convinced that the whole case had been grossly misrepresented and that the position taken up by the Holy Office was mistaken. He did not hesitate to make it known that those in high places in the Church had been misled. The ban was lifted and Padre Pio came down once more to the little public church to say Mass and hear confessions. Pius XI assumed a benevolent attitude towards this priest who was now close to his heart and he never showed any regret for having reversed his decision. The day on which the good news of Padre Pio's reinstatement reached the friary in San Giovanni Rotondo is one which will not easily be forgotten. The Father Provincial, in the presence of the whole community in the refectory, announced the joyful news to Padre Pio, while the friars applauded unanimously and cried out: "Long live the pope!" Padre Pio rose from his place, knelt before the Provincial and asked him in trembling tones to thank the pope on his behalf for this great grace.

On 12 March 1939 Cardinal Eugenio Pacelli ascended the papal throne, while in San Giovanni Rotondo Padre Pio was by that time involved in a vast spiritual ministry. Pius XII granted ample freedom to the stigmatised friar and rejoiced when he heard from many different sources of the great spiritual good accomplished by the humble Capuchin in his remote mountain friary.

Padre Pio's filial attitude towards the hierarchical Church

never wavered under any circumstances. He held firmly to traditional doctrine when many, even in ecclesiastical circles, tended to minimise authority and criticise the actions of Rome. For him, like St Catherine of Siena, the pope was the "sweet Christ on earth". Hence his attitude towards him was the same as his attitude to the Lord himself: sincere love with full and unconditional submission. He participated keenly in the pope's ˙sufferings and anxieties and on more than one occasion wrote to him to assure him of prayers and sufferings willingly offered for his intentions. The late Professor Enrico Medi, atomic scientist, told how Padre Pio confided to him one day in a low voice: "Enrico, tell the pope [Pius XII] that I'm ready to offer my life for him with immense joy." But the pope, when told of this, replied: "No, Professor, thank Padre Pio." Again, when the same eminent scientist asked Padre Pio what he was to tell the Pope (this time Paul VI) on his return to Rome, Padre Pio replied: "Tell him that I offer myself as a sacrifice for him and pray continually that the Lord may preserve him for a long time for his Church."

Padre Pio's first prayer in the morning was for the reigning pontiff. He would not listen to even the most innocent joke about the pope's authority or the authority of any superior. Towards the end of his life, when he sometimes expressed fears and doubts about the state of the Church, it was because he saw the danger of a progressive loss of the principle of authority, a too elastic interpretation of obedience, values in which he firmly believed.

With reference to the painful period through which he passed in the twenties and thirties, Padre Luigi of Avellino tells how he showed Padre Pio the order the superiors had received to send him to another region of Italy and describes Padre Pio's immediate reaction. He bowed his head and said "I am at your complete disposal. Let's leave at once. When I am with the Superior I am with God." During those years it had been rumoured several times that Padre Pio was to be transferred elsewhere, which gave rise to violent protests and rioting on the part of the local people. Actually the order for his transfer was withdrawn, but at the time it seemed quite probable that he would leave San Giovanni Rotondo. When the mayor of the town asked him if he was going to leave his people for good and said: "Will you leave by night, with the police, for who knows where?" Padre Pio answered very calmly: "If this order has been given I cannot do anything but carry out the will of my superiors. I am a son of obedience." We might say that obedience and loving submission to the voice of authority were second nature to this remarkable friar. When Rome decreed that he was not to answer the letters of those who wrote to him for guidance, to obtain favours or for any other motive, and it was added that further severe restrictions were to be issued later in his regard by the Roman Congregations, he was quite unperturbed and merely remarked: "Let them not delay too long. Let them tell us at once what we are to do."

He was very severe in his treatment of some of his friends who attacked authority on account of the measures taken against him during those difficult years. When Dr Festa included in a book a few words lacking in reverence for the Capuchin General whom he accused of failing to defend Padre Pio as he ought to have done, the latter wrote at once to the doctor and urged him vehemently to omit those words, threatening him with divine chastisement if he refused to comply with this request. The mayor of San Giovanni Rotondo, a devoted friend and defender of Padre Pio, went so far as to prepare a "white book" in the holy Capuchin's defence and tried to have it printed. When Padre Pio read the text he took the mayor by the back of the neck and in an outburst of holy anger shouted: "You fiend! Go and throw yourself at the feet of the Church instead of writing this nonsense. Don't dare to hurl yourself against your mother!"

A good deal has been said about his perfect spirit of obedience in an earlier chapter,[6] but we might quote many further examples here to illustrate his love for the Church. He never judged the actions of those placed over him. He merely bowed his head and obeyed, seeing in them the representatives of the Church he loved. No matter what changes were made in his usual manner of life as a result of the Church's decisions, he went about with a smile on his lips, invariably affable and cheerful. He can be seen as a living example of the sacrifice of a man's own will to that of authority. When they informed him that he must not take more than half-an-hour to say Mass he replied: "God knows that I want to say Mass just like any other priest, but I don't succeed." As we know quite well, he had special charisms which fitted him remarkably for the ministry to souls, but he himself wanted these charisms to be completely under the control of Church authority and he left it to God to arrange things after that. Who knows what immense fruits his obedience during that most painful trial obtained for the souls he loved so dearly?

A young friar who was rather full of himself sometimes argued with Padre Pio on the subject of the excessive severity of the Church in some instances and of "certain blunders" she made. Padre Pio remonstrated patiently with him. "The severity of the Church is always necessary in order to clarify our ideas," he said, "otherwise there would be chaos. There are many reasons for loving the Church, but in my opinion the mere fact that her severity down through the centuries has kept intact for us, at least in substance, the word of God and the Eucharist, ought to be sufficient to make us love her more than a mother." On another occasion he said to the same young friar: "Woe betide you if you don't place a bit of heart and brain at the service of the Church! It would be better for you not to be a friar." Then, with his eyes fixed on the little altar at which he had said Mass privately from 1931 to 1933 during the peak period of his painful segregation by order of the Holy See, he continued: "If I had not had holy Church behind me with her love and especially with her severity, perhaps I might have been drowned in a sea of doubt and uncertainty, or perhaps I might have become indifferent to the salvation of souls." Then raising his voice he said slowly: "For me the severity of the Church has been a refuge."[7]

One of the last acts of his life was to write a warm filial letter to Pope Paul VI[8] in which he said: "I offer you my prayers and daily sufferings as a small but sincere contribution on the part of the least of your sons, in order that God may comfort you with his grace to follow the straight and painful way in defence of eternal truth, which does not change with the passing of the years." Ten days later the holy stigmatist of Mount Gargano, a crucified son of holy Mother Church, breathed his last.

FOURTEEN

Our Lady in his Life

"Love our Lady. Recite the Rosary. May the Blessed Mother of God reign supreme over your hearts." These were the messages Padre Pio sent out continually to his spiritual sons and daughters near and far. This was the order he issued and the legacy he left to all, springing from his own ardent love for the Mother of God.

His love for Our Blessed Lady was a tender love, the love of a son who believes and hopes and trusts. It was no sentimental piety expressed in fine phrases, but a deep love resulting from constant meditation which gradually influenced his whole life. His own mother, Mamma Peppa, was deeply devoted to Mary the Mother of God. In the little rural centre in which he was born, devotion to the Madonna has been an outstanding characteristic of the people's religion for many centuries. In this respect the Pietrelcinese share a heritage common to the whole of southern Italy. Shrines to Our Blessed Lady, honoured under a great variety of titles, are to be found all over the region.

At a very early age Francesco Forgione, the future Padre Pio, joined his townsfolk in many pilgrimages to southern Marian shrines: to Montevergine high up in the mountains about thirty miles from his home and to the shrine of Our Lady of Pompeii in the vicinity of Naples. One of the essential components of his spirituality in later life was this deep devotion to Mary, the roots of which we can trace to the truly Marian atmosphere in which his early years were spent in Pietrelcina. Little anecdotes have come to us, either from his early companions or from his own reminiscences, which show how really devoted his people were to the Mother of God.

When young Francesco was leaving his home for the Capuchin novitiate, the only gift he received from his mother was a huge rosary beads, which is kept today in the archives

of the Postulation in San Giovanni Rotondo. These treasured
rosary beads and a picture of "our own Madonna" as he
called Our Lady Liberatrix, accompanied Padre Pio all through
life. The title Our Lady Liberatrix (*Madonna della Libera*)
goes back very far in the history of that region.[1] In the
seventh century, when the little dukedom of Benevento was
besieged by the Byzantine Emperor Constans II, the saintly
local bishop who is known today as San Barbato led his
people in prayer to Our Blessed Lady with the intention of
freeing *(liberare)* the city from the fury of the Greeks. Their
prayer was heard and San Barbato spread devotion to Our
Lady under the title of Liberatrix. In his youth Padre Pio
venerated the Mother of God under this title, which has
rather special overtones in Pietrelcina even today. The little
town celebrates a feast in honour of its Madonna more than
once during the year, in grateful thanks for past favours.

In 1854 the town was struck by an epidemic of cholera.
At the beginning of December it seemed as if the population
would be wiped out completely. "Dozens were dying each
day," says the local historian. "As men walked along the
streets they suddenly fell down and died on the spot." On
3 December the whole population gathered in and around the
church to pray at the feet of their beloved Madonna. Then
her statue was carried through the streets in the firm hope
that death would flee before her, and in point of fact, as the
chronicler tells us, "from that day the disease claimed no
more victims and the people were convinced that Our Lady
of the Libera had obtained this grace for their town".

Liberation from cholera "was not the only act of benevolence shown by Our Lady towards us", the Pietrelcinese will
tell you. "She has come to our assistance when the fields
needed water and when our crops were threatened by hail-
storms. The people in the next town, Paduli, say that we have
the Madonna within easy reach."

There are still a few people alive who remember the "grace"
of Palm Sunday 1906. The church in the castle district was
packed for high Mass at noon. Suddenly the sky darkened
and within the church it was as if night had fallen. Then an
exceptionally violent thunderstorm made it impossible to

hear the priest's words, and what is more, it rained clay and stones, as the people will tell you. The terrified congregation cried out and wept and nobody could leave the church. It seemed as if the end of the world had come. Then fervent supplications went up from the crowd to Jesus and his Blessed Mother. Suddenly the storm ended, the sun came out and all were able to walk to their homes. The explanation of this phenomenon only reached Pietrelcina some days later. The solid substance which had rained down on them consisted of ashes and cinders, the result of a violent eruption of Vesuvius over fifty miles away.

While the historic event of 1854 is commemorated on 3 December with a solemn Mass, sermon and procession, the principal feast of the Liberatrix takes place in August and lasts a full three days. A special committee of "Masters of the Feast" is appointed to arrange the programme. The committee is chosen from among the more mature members of the community by secret ballot. Padre Pio's own father never tired of telling how he was chosen at nineteen years of age. When his name came out at the first ballot it was considered an error, so a second and then a third ballot took place, which confirmed the result of the first. As an old man, *Zi' Grazio* would say with tears in his eyes: "Imagine being a Master of the Feast at nineteen years of age!"

Although there is feasting and music in the central piazza and the inevitable display of fireworks without which no southern Italian festa would be complete, the feast of Our Lady Liberatrix is an essentially religious celebration. A special preacher arrives for the three days and the preparatory novena is always well attended. In Padre Pio's letters, written during his prolonged stay in Pietrelcina as a young priest, there is frequent mention of this celebration and Padre Agostino, his confessor at the time, was invited more than once to preach for the occasion.

The wooden statue of Our Lady Liberatrix, the work of a seventeenth-century Neapolitan artist, was formerly venerated in a church on the outskirts of the town. When this church was devastated by a landslide the image was taken to the parochial church where it can be seen today. It was cleverly

restored and repainted in 1965 and on 17 July 1966 the
Vatican Chapter assigned to it a golden crown in recognition
of the part it had played for centuries in the people's devotion to Mary. In a solemn ceremony on 6 August 1966, the
diadem was placed on the head of the Madonna by Mgr
Raffaele Calabria, Archbishop of Benevento. Padre Pio, in
his friary at San Giovanni Rotondo many miles away, rejoiced
along with his townsfolk. Some of the older folk in Pietrelcina
tell how they used to see him as "a young Capuchin priest
of thoughtful and ascetical appearance, transfigured before
the statue of his beloved Madonna" as he prayed there each
day during his enforced residence at home.

Padre Pio contemplated Our Lady within God's plan for
the salvation of mankind. Close to her he felt closer to Christ
our Lord. On 6 May 1913 he wrote to Padre Agostino:

> This most tender Mother, in her great mercy, wisdom and goodness,
> has been pleased to punish me in a most exalted manner by pouring
> so many and such great graces into my heart that when I am in
> her presence and in that of Jesus I am compelled to exclaim: "Where
> am I? Who is this who is near me?" I am all aflame although there
> is no fire. I feel myself held fast and bound to the Son by means of
> this Mother, without seeing the chains which bind me so tightly.

He always kept the picture of Our Lady Liberatrix on the
wall of his cell. He used to look tenderly towards it before
taking his frugal repast, before going to rest and each time
he returned to his cell weary and fatigued after his Mass or
confessions. He was to look towards his *Mammina,* his "dear
little Mother" with great tenderness just before his eyes
closed in death.

His love for Mary found expression in ardent, confident,
uninterrupted prayer. Who could count the number of Rosar-
ies he recited in the course of his long life? Padre Pietro
Tartaglia, Guardian of the friary in San Giovanni Rotondo in
1978, said:

> I can see him today as he appeared to me when I was a youngster.
> It was beautiful to see him there in the silence of his cell when we
> Capuchin aspirants went to him for confession. The dim light gave a
> mystical touch to his emaciated but radiant countenance. Near him

was . . . a little statue of Our Lady and he spoke to us about her and taught us to love her. At a certain hour he used to walk in the friary garden, absorbed in his sufferings and his love while the beads slipped through the fingers of his wounded hands. And how full and ardent was his voice when he recited the Angelus with the others.

The Rosary and the Angelus: two time-honoured forms of devotion to the Blessed Virgin which have tended to disappear in recent years. Vatican II said nothing to downgrade these devotional practices, yet many over-zealous efforts at conciliar reform seem to have stifled them. Is the ecumenical effort in many places perhaps pushing Our Lady into the background, or even behind the scenes, so as not to place obstacles in the path of Christian unity? Pope Paul VI did not appear to support this trend. As recently as 1974, in his apostolic exhortation *Marialis Cultus,* he set forth in the clearest terms the value of the Rosary and the Angelus and strongly recommended them to the faithful.

. . . the Rosary draws from the Gospel the presentation of the mysteries and its main formulas. As it moves from the Angel's joyful greeting and the Virgin's pious assent, the Rosary takes its inspiration from the Gospel to suggest the attitude with which the faithful should recite it. In the harmonious succession of Hail Marys the Rosary puts before us once more a fundamental mystery of the Gospel, the Incarnation of the Word, contemplated at the decisive moment of the Annunciation to Mary. The Rosary is thus a Gospel prayer, as pastors and scholars like to define it more today perhaps than in the past . . . The Rosary considers . . . the principal salvific events accomplished in Christ, from his virginal conception and the mysteries of his childhood to the culminating moments of the Passover, the blessed Passion and the glorious Resurrection, to the effects of this on the infant Church on the day of Pentecost, and on the Virgin Mary when she was assumed body and soul into her heavenly home . . .[2]

What we have to say about the Angelus is meant to be only a simple but earnest exhortation to continue its traditional recitation wherever and whenever possible. The Angelus does not need to be revised, because of its simple structure, its biblical character, its historical origin which links it to the prayer for peace and safety, and its quasi-liturgical rhythm which sanctifies different moments of the day, and because it reminds us of the Paschal Mystery. In recalling the Incarnation of the Son of God we pray that we may be led "through his Passion and Cross to the glory of his Resurrection". These factors ensure that the Angelus despite the passing of centuries retains an unaltered value and an intact freshness.[3]

Padre Pio was already dead six years when this document appeared. We cannot help imagining how he who was so assiduous in his recitation of both the Rosary and the Angelus would have welcomed Pope Paul's words on the subject. Those whose good fortune it was to live close to him or to visit San Giovanni Rotondo during his lifetime cannot easily forget the intense fervour with which he recited the Angelus in their midst when the Ave Maria rang out from the belfry of his friary, or the touching tones of his voice as he led the Rosary at evening devotions. To a lady who asked him for a few words which would contain a programme of life Padre Pio's characteristically brief reply was: "My child, the Rosary."

With Padre Pio, love for Our Lady meant continual imitation of her virtues. To quote once more Padre Pietro Tartaglia:

> Reproducing her virtues, with her help, he drew ever closer to his Lord and Master, so very close as to be transformed into him. His imitation of Mary meant, in the first place, imitation of her humility. For him that humility was a constant interior torment, a slow and painful agony, the anguish of not knowing whether he was corresponding to divine grace or not. You could read that deep humility on his face even when he was surrounded by enthusiastic crowds who believed in him, who trusted in his prayers to obtain innumerable graces. On such occasions he remained in deeply humble recollection. It was this profound and Mary-like humility that made him accept cheerfully and in dignified silence the misunderstandings, humiliations, calumnies and moral sufferings which were showered upon him in abundance. His deep love for the Mother of God induced him to unite with her in utter donation, in the continual sacrifice of a loving victim, by excruciating sufferings without an instant's respite.

Padre Pio wrote to Padre Benedetto in July 1915: "May the most holy Virgin obtain for us a love of the cross, a love of pain and suffering, and may she who was the first to practise the Gospel in all its perfection before it was written, enable us and stimulate us to follow her example. We must make every effort to walk close to her, since there is no other path leading to life except the path followed by our Mother." His love engendered cheerful and boundless trust: "Hasn't God placed all his graces in Our Lady's hands?" he wrote to Padre Agostino around the same time. "He has placed the cause of my salvation and the ultimate victory in her hands. Protected and guided by so tender a Mother, I will continue to fight as long as God wills, full of confidence in this Mother and certain that I shall never succumb."

This same love prompted him to practise continual mortification. He implored his spiritual director to let him abstain from eating fruit on Wednesdays and asked him to suggest a means of pleasing this Blessed Mother in all things and at all times. He became an apostle of the love of Mary: "I would like to have a voice loud enough to invite the sinners of the whole world to love Our Lady." Padre Pio *had* a voice that was powerful even when he was silent. It was a voice that touched the depths of people's hearts, that dug down into their consciences to torment and shake those who were too easygoing. It was a voice that was terrible as the crashing of thunder in the night, yet sweet as a caress, a voice that brought people to their knees and raised them up, a voice that consoled and dispensed forgiveness.

From the day on which he became a priest he always preferred to say Mass at Our Lady's altar, first in Pietrelcina and later in San Giovanni Rotondo. Moreover, the Mass he celebrated most frequently was the Mass of the Immaculate Conception. When his eyesight was failing and he could read the altar missal only with great difficulty, he was dispensed from saying the Mass of the day and allowed to say the Mass of Our Lady or the Mass for the Dead.

Twice it would seem that Mary Immaculate intervened to save him when he was close to death. The first of these occasions was in 1911, when at twenty-four years of age he was sent to the friary in Venafro and became so ill there that he had to be accompanied back to his own home. The very next day, which was the feast of the Immaculate Conception, to the surprise of all he sang Mass just as if he had not been ill at all.

From his earliest years Padre Pio cherished a tender filial love for the Blessed Virgin honoured as Our Lady of Pompeii and on many occasions he went to her shrine near the ruined city. In 1901, at the age of fourteen, he made a pilgrimage there with seven of his schoolmates accompanied by their teacher. His mother does not seem to have been very happy about that trip and complained about it in a letter to her husband who had emigrated to America to earn some extra money for his son's studies. When his father wrote to young Francesco from America the boy answered him in order to justify his trip to Pompeii: "As regards my going to Pompeii, you are quite right. However, you ought to remember that next year, please God, all holidays and amusements will be over for me when I abandon this life to embrace a better one." Reading between the lines we can gather that young Francesco went to Pompeii to recommend to his "very dear Mother" his forthcoming entry to the Capuchins and to place his religious life under her protection.

While obliged to serve in the army as a young friar, he availed of every opportunity to run down to Pompeii from Naples where he was stationed, to "say a few words" to his beloved Madonna. When he was released from the army for six months' convalescence in 1917, we find him again making the trip there to thank Our Blessed Lady for this grace. During those years he was tireless in his prayers to the Virgin of Pompeii in novena after novena for a return to conventual life, though still obliged by delicate health to remain in his own home. He also prayed to her for what he called his "speedy departure", by which he meant death. He appealed to his directors and to others bound to him by spiritual ties to recite novenas to Our Lady of Pompeii for his intentions. It was to the Virgin Mother of God honoured under this title that he also directed his fervent prayers to be exonerated from military service, which for him was physical and spiritual torture. He was granted a return to his community and a discharge from the army, but the "speedy departure" was deferred for half a century. Even then, in 1968, when he realised he was dying, it was to Our Lady of Pompeii that he turned, to thank her from the depths of his heart.

World War I was drawing to a close when Our Blessed Lady appeared in Fatima. At that time Padre Pio was undergoing the harsh experience of life in a military barracks. As an unequalled Marian devotee he meditated deeply on the Fatima message, and in response to Our Lady's invitation prayed without ceasing that the divine mercy might prevail over the divine justice. There is an undeniable link between the apparitions in Fatima and the justice of God and between this justice and the victim state, the state of those souls who offer themselves in reparation for men's offences against God, to placate the divine justice. Hence we can establish a loving relationship between Padre Pio, one of these victims for souls, and Our Lady of Fatima. Through her intercession he obtained a genuine miracle for himself, he who had been the channel of so many miraculous graces for others. He had been suffering from pleurisy from 5 May 1959 and the doctors had diagnosed a tumour on the lung, so that his life hung in the balance. Just then the pilgrim statue of Our Lady of Fatima was being transported all over Italy in the memorable *Peregrinatio Mariae*. On 5 August, in the final days of the pilgrimage, the statue was brought to San Giovanni Rotondo in a helicopter, which circled over the Capuchin friary. Before the image departed, Padre Pio addressed a fervent prayer from his sick-bed to Our Blessed Lady in the following words: "My dear Mother, since your arrival in Italy I have been reduced to helplessness by this illness, and now that you are leaving have you nothing to give me?" At once he felt a mysterious strength invade his body and he exclaimed to his confrères: "I'm cured!" Shortly afterwards a local paper in Foggia published an article asking why the Pilgrim Virgin should have been taken to San Giovanni Rotondo and not to the famous shrine of St Michael in Monte Santangelo higher up on Mount Gargano, a place of pilgrimage for centuries. When one of the Capuchins drew Padre Pio's attention to this complaint, he replied quite simply: "Our Lady came here because she wanted to cure Padre Pio!"

Padre Pio's relations with Our Blessed Lady were quite exceptional. He used to speak of being surfeited with graces by her. "She treats me as if I were her only child on the face of the earth," he said. Padre Raffaele, an elderly friar who lived close to him for many years, asked him one day why he didn't visit Loreto. "Because," said Padre Pio, "if I went there I'd die of devotion." A younger friar, Padre Eusebio, speaking to him about Our Lady one day, said suddenly: "You see her, don't you?" Taken off his guard Padre Pio admitted this. "She comes to me whenever I need her," he said. Others around him who were deeply aware of his close union with Our Lady often sought to extract some further confidence from him. Said one of these: "Padre, does Our Lady ever come to your cell?" His reply was surprising: "Ask me, instead, does she ever leave my cell." On several occasions he confided to his intimates that the Blessed Virgin remained beside him while he heard confessions.

It has been said that the artist who wants to paint the most realistic portrait of Padre Pio would do well to depict a humble Capuchin friar, crucified by suffering and love, with rosary beads between his fingers. This is how his fellow friars were accustomed to see him up to the last day of his life. On that day, when he could no longer speak, he still clasped the beads between his bloodless fingers, while from his lips which were about to close for ever came the repeated feeble murmur: "Jesus! . . . Mary! . . . Jesus! . . . Mary!" His final word, then, was the sweet name of Mary the Mother of God, his greatest love after his crucified Saviour.[4]

FIFTEEN

Witnesses to the Stigmata

During the first meeting on the spirituality of Padre Pio, held in San Giovanni Rotondo in 1972 and already mentioned in Chapter 13, one of the most interesting lectures was delivered by Father George Cruchon, SJ, professor of Pastoral Psychology at the Pontifical Gregorian University in Rome.[1] Professor Cruchon made ample use of the reports submitted by the various doctors who were sent to examine Padre Pio during the year immediately following the appearance of those painful wounds in his flesh. The medical reports are long and detailed, and while this writer has read them attentively, it will not be possible to give more than a synthesis of the doctors' findings in the present context.

Before going on to consider the medical evidence itself, Father Cruchon pointed out that it is only in the souls of a very few privileged persons that love for Jesus crucified becomes so strong as to seek identification with his sufferings. Even in the case of souls who experience such intense spiritual suffering, there are very few instances in which it is accompanied by external marks or wounds. Padre Pio makes it clear to us in his writings that while he ardently desired to suffer for Christ and with him, he never had the slightest desire to see those sufferings externalised in his flesh and made visible to those around him. He yearned to be identified with Christ in his ministry to souls and in his supreme sacrifice, but he certainly had no desire to receive the stigmata. In a letter to Padre Benedetto in October 1918, a month after the appearance of those bleeding wounds, he revealed how earnestly he wished to be relieved, not of the pain which he gladly endured, but of "these external signs, which are an indescribable and unbearable humiliation to me".

The Church is normally very cautious in recognising miracles or extraordinary phenomena in those whom popular opinion is quick to consider saints and wonder-workers. Out of more than 300 cases of alleged stigmatisation, she has not recognised more than about sixty. It was quite natural that the sensational reports emanating in 1919 from San Giovanni Rotondo and the furore which resulted around the person of Padre Pio at the time should lead to rigorous investigation by ecclesiastical authority. It was also natural that more than one illustrious member of the medical profession should be sent to examine the phenomenon.

The first to be entrusted with this onerous task was Dr Luigi Romanelli, chief surgeon at the civilian hospital in Barletta, near Bari. Five times in the course of a little over a year, from May 1919 to July 1920, Dr Romanelli who was a fervent Catholic, examined Padre Pio at the request of the Capuchin General. Apart from the scientific report on his findings, he expressed to the local superiors the happiness he experienced close to Padre Pio, when he was favoured like many others with an inebriating perfume. He was proud to be the first doctor to observe what he described as "that living miracle" and he added that he should therefore "like to be kept in mind whenever Padre Pio might be in need of earthly assistance". In his report to the Provincial he described in detail the wounds as he had observed them in Padre Pio's hands and feet and side, their size, shape and colour, their exact anatomical position and the appearance of the flesh and skin around those wounds, which he had probed repeatedly. He described the wound in Padre Pio's side as "a cut, more than two inches in length".

Dr Romanelli went on to state in his report that these could not be classified as wounds of an ordinary nature, for even a person with no medical skill whatever, he said, could see that they showed no sign either of festering or of the healing process which ordinarily sets in in the case of a healthy wound. He utterly excluded the possibility of self-inflicted wounds, which would follow the natural course either of suppuration or healing. Padre Pio's wounds, he stated, had remained in the very same state over a period of many months, a phenomenon which human science could not explain.[2]

Towards the end of July 1920, at the request of Father Venantius of Lisle-en-Rigault, General of the Capuchins, an eminent doctor from Rome University, Professor Amico Bignami, carried out a further medical examination on Padre Pio, after which he too submitted a detailed report on the friar's general health and on his wounds. His description of the five wounds corresponded in the main to that already submitted by Dr Romanelli. He found that Padre Pio had been using iodine as a disinfectant which, as the young friar himself told the doctor, helped to arrest the bleeding. Dr Bignami, unlike Dr Romanelli, was a professed atheist. He was perplexed by the nature of the wounds and suggested three possible explanations: (a) that they were produced artificially by Padre Pio himself; (b) that they were caused by a disease (unspecified); (c) that they were partly artificial and partly the result of a disease. He concluded that there was nothing to show that they had been produced by anything but disease or the use of some chemical such as tincture of iodine.

At the end of his examination Dr Bignami ordered the Provincial to forbid Padre Pio the use of any medicines and to take all such things away from his room. Moreover, before leaving San Giovanni Rotondo, he left instructions that the wounds were to be bandaged and sealed in the presence of several witnesses who were to examine the seals each morning for eight consecutive days to make sure they had not been tampered with. At the end of this period the witnesses were to remove the bandages and report whether the wounds had healed or not. Three exemplary Capuchins were chosen for this delicate task. Padre Gerardo Di Flumeri, in a note on the stigmata,[3] tells us in detail how Dr Bignami's instructions were carried out and gives us the text of the report submitted by the three Capuchins at the end of the eight days.

We, the undersigned, state under oath that we received from Padre Pietro of Ischitella [Provincial] the order to bandage the wounds of the Capuchin friar, Pio of Pietrelcina, and that we observed: (a) that the wounds remained in the same state during the eight days, except for the last day, on which they turned bright red; (b) each day, as can be seen from the bandages we have kept, all five wounds bled. On the final day the bleeding was more profuse, so that while Padre Pio was saying Mass we were obliged to send a fresh bandage to the altar to stem the blood which was streaming down the back of his hands. It is to be noted that in bandaging his wounds we used no medicine. Although we trusted Padre Pio completely, in order to forestall any suspicions we removed the bottle of iodine he kept in his room.

This document bears the signature of the three Capuchins.

In his profound study already quoted, Father Cruchon SJ comments: "We can accept Dr Bignami's hypothesis during the period in which Padre Pio used iodine. But the bleeding after eight days of sealed bandaging and the persistence of healthy bleeding wounds to which iodine was no longer applied, during fifty years, has yet to be explained."[4]

In October 1919 the Capuchin General arranged for a further medical examination, this time by Dr Giorgio Festa, who made his first examination of the stigmatised friar in October and sent his report about a month later to the General. Before going up to San Giovanni Rotondo, Dr Festa saw the Provincial in Foggia and read a number of documents regarding Padre Pio which he found most important from the medical point of view.

Doctor Festa's report highlights many aspects of Padre Pio's personality before passing on to an account of the wounds as he found them. He was a guest in the friary and had occasion to note the young priest's behaviour in community, his gentle smiling countenance, his cheerfulness and obvious intelligence, his ready participation in many a witty conversation at recreation. He also remarked that Padre Pio seemed transformed whenever the conversation turned to spiritual topics and he was struck by the young friar's utter sincerity. He saw how little food he ate and noted his capacity, despite this fact, to devote a great many hours to hearing confessions and listening to visitors.

Articles by well-known neuropathologists at that time pointed out that hysteria can produce wounds or lesions of the skin. There were those who maintained that except for St Francis of Assisi and St Catherine of Siena, most cases of alleged stigmatisation could be accounted for in this way. Dr Festa, who examined Padre Pio, refuted emphatically the hysteria theory. As a result of his long interviews and close questioning of Padre Pio he stated that he found complete balance and perfect harmony between the functions of his nervous system and his mental faculties. As in the case of the previous medical examiners, Dr Festa gave a detailed account of the five wounds which he had examined minutely. His report is much longer and more detailed than those of the two doctors who carried out the previous examinations. He considers various cases recorded by the medical profession in which superficial wounds have been observed in neuropathic patients whose psychic and mental faculties were more or less perturbed or who were hypnotised or strongly influenced in some other way. His emphatic conclusion is that the class-ification of Padre Pio among such cases is not to be enter-tained for an instant and can be completely refuted on the basis of his perfect mental balance, the consistency he showed in all his acts and words, his total consecration to prayer, meditation and the good of all those who approached him. Dr Festa's final word, in view of the medical evidence, is that the origin of Padre Pio's bleeding wounds is something which we are far from being able to explain.[5] Reference has been made in Chapter 7 to the operation performed by Dr Festa on Padre Pio over five years later, when the latter was suffering from a serious hernia. On that occasion the surgeon had a further opportunity to observe the five wounds which had undergone no change in the course of those years.

Leaving aside the scientific reports submitted by these eminent doctors, there are numerous witnesses to the genuine and persistent existence of those bleeding wounds. During his public Mass over several decades, when devout crowds pressed around the altar, the wounds in his hands were clearly visible when he raised them during the Canon. Many devout residents in San Giovanni Rotondo have frequently spoken of seeing his half-gloved hands stained with blood. We have, moreover, the reliable testimony of a number of the friars who assisted him at the altar and during the day and who were accustomed to the sight of those wounded hands. On some occasions during his last years they also saw the wounds in his feet and side, when he required assistance in his cell. An issue of *The Voice of Padre Pio*[6] carries the accounts of some of the friars who were closest to him during those years, and it is worthwhile summarising them here.

Padre Alessio Parente, who is well known to English-speaking visitors to San Giovanni Rotondo, assisted Padre Pio for a number of years towards the end of his life. He relates how one morning in February 1968 Padre Pio asked to be left alone for about ten minutes to attend to his "own affairs", by which he meant that he wanted to change his mittens and the little bandages covering his wounds, as he often did at that hour.

> I took some fresh bandages from the cupboard, placed them on the table and left him alone. When he failed to ring for me after more than ten minutes I was rather anxious at the delay, so I went to his door and asked if I might come in. He replied in a beseeching tone: "Come in, my son, and help me." I found him lying on the bed, his left hand dangling while he held onto the bed with his right. His hands were bare, one mitten was on the table, the other on the floor along with the blood-soaked bandages. I was alarmed at first, then I put my arms around him and sat him up on the bed. He had had a bout of dizziness, something to which he was subject . . . I had always wanted to see his wounds and that day I had the good fortune to see them and confirm that they really existed . . . The wounds on the back of his hands were almost half an inch deep, while those on the palm were covered with a wide thick scab. In the wounds there was partially dried blood which I removed with great care. I didn't remove it all, for I saw that every touch caused him to wince with pain. I dried his hands thoroughly, disinfected the mittens with camphorated spirits and put them on his hands.

On 12 April 1972 Padre Eusebio, who had been Padre Pio's assistant and secretary from 1960 to 1965, gave (to Father George Cruchon SJ) an account of how he had seen the side wound, in the form of an oblique cross. He told how, at about ten o'clock one evening a loud noise came from Padre Pio's cell and he was heard calling for help. Father Guardian and Father Eusebio hurried to the spot and found that Padre Pio had fallen to the floor . . . It was necessary on that occasion to change his habit and shirt. The wound in his side was clean and blood and serum oozed from it.

Padre Pellegrino, another of his assistants, signed a declaration in February 1969 with regard to Padre Pio's wounds and their gradual closing during the last three years of his life.

> I often saw the wounds in Padre Pio's hands. There was a wound in the centre of the hand, covered with scabs. Only once did I see the wound in his side. It was between two and three inches long and more than an inch wide and it seemed to go very deep. At that moment it was not bleeding . . . During the last three years I was able to observe how the wounds were gradually disappearing. However, his feet were very painful, so much so that I was in a panic whenever I had to put on his sandals. It was enough to touch his instep ever so slightly to cause him great pain, which was evident at once from the way he winced . . .

> Four or five months before his death the wounds were still open but the bleeding had gradually diminished. The faithful who assisted at his Mass were aware of this and also observed how Padre Pio, who had always tried to hide the wounds in his hands with the sleeves of the alb, now allowed his hands to be seen . . . On 22 September 1968, while he celebrated his last Mass, two scabs fell from his hands. On the morning of the 23rd just after his death, while Doctor Sala and myself were laying him out, the last scab fell from his left hand. It was then that Dr Sala, the Guardian and myself realised that the wounds had disappeared from his side and feet and hands, leaving no scars. Padre Giacomo took photographs.

The disappearance of every trace of wounds which had bled for fifty years presents a problem. A deep and lasting wound which has damaged the tissue always leaves a scar, but here there was no trace at all. Dr Sala, who was Padre Pio's physician during his last years, signed the following declaration in 1969:

> Padre Pio had circular wounds, almost an inch wide, on both sides of his hands and feet. It was possible to see his hands quite well on certain occasions, and the wounds were visible: clean, exuding bright red blood and surrounded by irregular layers of clotted blood. There was no sign of inflammation and no discharge of pus. The edges of the wounds were quite clean. The wound in his side, the shape of a lozenge was obviously deep, with clean edges, free from scabs. Hands and feet, especially the left foot, were greatly swollen but not discoloured. A few months before his death his feet were no longer swollen and the wounds already described were not to be seen. He

still bore traces of the wounds up to the day of his death, but the skin had changed colour, the scabs had almost disappeared and the wounds on the back of his hands were no longer visible.

Dr Sala, who was present during his brief agony, continues:

During his agony, his left hand still bore a scab which was removed when he died. Ten minutes after death, his hands, feet and chest were photographed by a friar in the presence of four members of the community and myself. There was no sign of any wound, nor were there any scars on feet or hands, back or front, or on the chest. The skin on those parts of the body was the same as the rest, soft and resilient. When a finger was pressed to the spot there was no sign of a hollow in the flesh beneath it, nor any evidence of cut, laceration, wound or inflammation. These things [concludes the doctor] must be considered as outside all typology of clinical action and of a character beyond the natural.[7]

All of these witnesses were quoted by Father Cruchon in his memorable lecture during the 1972 meeting, and this chapter may be fittingly ended with the final remarks of this learned Jesuit.

What more is needed to confirm the authenticity of the stigmata, especially when these wounds were integrated in a life completely dedicated to God, to prayer and the service of others? This was no life of secluded contemplation. It was a faithful life, free from any neurotic outbursts, a life of patience and heroic obedience in face of disciplinary measures taken against him, a life of exemplary charity in his community. Padre Pio's whole life might be summed up in the words of St Paul to the Colossians: "Now I rejoice in my sufferings for your sake, and in my flesh I complete what is lacking in Christ's afflictions for the sake of his body, that is, the Church" *(Col 1:24)*.

SIXTEEN

The Voice of the Hierarchy

English-speaking devotees of Padre Pio, even those who have paid more than one visit to his tomb and to the friary which witnessed the remarkable events of his life, are probably unaware of the tributes which popes and bishops have paid to the stigmatised friar of Mount Gargano. From time to time such statements have appeared in the Italian journal published by the friars, while many testimonies of visiting prelates are also to be found in various volumes of the visitors' book, kept among the records of the friary. Occasionally in the precincts of the church one finds a tribute in the form of an inscription in Italian, which means little to most English-speaking visitors. It may therefore be useful to bring together in this chapter the more important of these authoritative statements from various sources, so as to present a general picture of the esteem in which Padre Pio was held by so many Church dignitaries, starting with the popes who spoke out in his favour after he had received the stigmata.

Pope Paul VI undoubtedly held Padre Pio in great veneration. We give a free translation here of the pope's eloquent testimony on a particular occasion, the text of which appears in Italian on a tablet near Padre Pio's tomb. The occasion was 20 February 1971, when the Holy Father received in audience the Father General of the Capuchin order, Father Paschal Rywalski, with his Definitors. During that audience Father Rywalski presented the pope with the first volume of Padre Pio's letters which had just appeared in Italian. His Holiness then addressed a warm exhortation to the group, urging them to seek out in their apostolate particularly those who were less willing to hear of religion. "Perhaps they'll deride you in the first instance," said the pope, "but perhaps the miraculous success which Padre Pio knew will also be yours. Look how famous he became! Look at the clientèle he gathered around him from all parts of the world! Why was this? Was it, perhaps, because he was a philosopher, or a great scholar, or because he had means at his disposal? It was because he said Mass with humility, heard confessions from morning till night and because he was a representative of Our Lord marked with the imprint of his wounds." When the General remarked that Padre Pio was a man of prayer, the pope replied: "He was a man of prayer and *suffering.*"[1]

As Archbishop of Milan, Cardinal Montini had already spoken highly of Padre Pio, expressing the opinion that "one Mass celebrated by Padre Pio was as good as a mission". In 1960, for the fiftieth anniversary of the holy Capuchin's ordination, the future Pope Paul wrote him a letter in which he expressed his "confidence and deference". "I hear that you are soon to celebrate the fiftieth anniversary of your priestly ordination," the letter began, "and I venture to congratulate you in the Lord on the immense graces which have been bestowed on you and dispensed by you." Padre Pio responded to this warm interest and appreciation by his filial devotion to the Vicar of Christ until the day of his death and by offering his intense sufferings during those last years for the solution of the grave problems which grieved and tormented the heart of the pope.[2] When Pope Paul was informed in September 1968 of Padre Pio's death, he sent a telegram of sympathy to the community and assured them of his prayers "that the Lord might grant his faithful servant an eternal crown". Just one month later, when he received the Capuchin fathers assembled for their General Chapter, he spoke to them in warm tones of their venerable confrère. He assured them that the austere form of Franciscan rule embraced by the Capuchin order had always found favour in the eyes of the Church and of the world, which recognised something particularly attractive in it. Immediately afterwards the pope's thoughts turned to Padre Pio and he spoke of the devotion which had surrounded this exemplary Capuchin in particular.[3]

Reference has already been made, in Chapter 13, to the esteem expressed by earlier popes for the stigmatised friar. During the eighty years of his life the Throne of Peter was occupied by seven different popes. In early childhood Francesco Forgione frequently heard mention of Pope Leo XIII. The pope of his early years as a Capuchin was the great Saint Pius X to whom he was particularly devoted. The five popes who followed were familiar with the activity of this extra-ordinary priest and expressed their opinion of him in no uncertain terms. As we have already seen, the only pope he ever saw in person was Benedict XV, on the occasion of his one visit to Rome in May 1917. It was towards the end of this pontificate that Padre Pio received the stigmata and Pope Benedict's words in praise of him have already been reported in Chapter 13.

What has always been considered the most painful period of Padre Pio's life occurred when the Milanese Pope, Pius XI, occupied the See of Peter. As we have already seen in the chapter just mentioned, this pope realised before long that the accusations which had caused so much suffering to the holy friar of San Giovanni Rotondo and those closest to him were unfounded, and it was he who restored full freedom to Padre Pio in his priestly ministry. Speaking at the time to a Capuchin bishop, Mgr Cornelius S. Cuccarollo,.the pope said: "You Capuchin fathers will be happy now that Padre Pio has been reinstated in his ministry." Then he added: "This is a very rare if not a unique case in history."[4]

Pius XII, during the nineteen years of his pontificate (1939-1958) witnessed the blossoming of Padre Pio's two providential projects, the Casa Sollievo della Sofferenza (his hospital) and the "prayer groups". He expressed repeat-edly his high opinion of the friar of Mount Gargano, to whom in 1957 he granted the faculty to act as administrator of the hospital for the remainder of his life. Pope Pius XII is reported to have said to the famous sculptor Francesco Messina: "Padre Pio is a great saint . . . he is certainly a saintly man." He repeated similar words of praise of their confrère to a group of missionaries from Foggia who were about to leave for Africa in 1949. This pope frequently asked Padre Pio's particular prayers and in February 1949 requested him to say Mass "for a special intention of mine". In an audience granted to a group of French pilgrims who were going on from Rome to San Giovanni Rotondo, the pope said: "Yes, go there, it will be good for you."[5] Pope Pius XII also sent a niece and nephew of his own to receive their first communion from Padre Pio's hands instead of his and on another occasion the pope's sister visited Padre Pio.

Pope John XXIII during his short reign instructed his Secretary of State, Cardinal Tardini, to convey "special words of approbation" for the development and projected extension of Padre Pio's hospital and for the "tireless zeal" of its founder.[6] Pope John's pontificate was to be marked by new investigations into events which were taking place in San Giovanni Rotondo, which caused Padre Pio further deep suffering. While authorising this painful enquiry, Pope John stated that "since Padre Pio's name was already resounding throughout the world" it was necessary to "prevent anything which might damage that name". At the beginning of his pontificate he had sent Padre Pio a special blessing. To a priest in audience who mentioned that he came from Foggia, Pope John exclaimed, raising his hands: "You have the great Padre Pio down there." In a moment of difficulty and anxiety, in receiving the Archbishop of Manfredonia, Mgr Andrea Cesarano, Pope John said spontaneously: "Tell Padre Pio also to continue his prayers!"

From 1963 to the day of his death in 1968, Padre Pio was no longer subjected to any Roman investigations. Pope Paul VI, who had been his devotee for years, looked on him with particular benevolence and spoke of him frequently, as we have already seen.

During the later years of Padre Pio's life many cardinals were seen at his friary. Cardinal Federico Tedeschini, who visited the new church and crowned the image of Our Blessed Lady there in July 1959, was accompanied by the Bishop of Foggia, at that time Mgr Paolo Carta. The latter recalls how impressed the Cardinal was by the humility and holiness of the stigmatised friar and how he continued to repeat as they drove down the mountainside: "Padre Pio leads to God, he leads to God!"

The Franciscan cardinal, Mgr Ferdinand G. Antonelli, celebrated Mass at Padre Pio's tomb in October 1975 and left a precious message in the visitors' book. His testimony is of particular importance, since he was for many years Prefect of what is now known as the Congregation for the Causes of Saints. "The fame of a person's holiness is the starting point from which the Church proceeds with a cause for beatification." he wrote. "The fame of Padre Pio's holiness has spread to a unique extent in our days." A few days later His Eminence wrote from Rome to the Guardian in San Giovanni Rotondo:

> I still have a vivid impression before my eyes of the Mass I celebrated in the crypt where Padre Pio's remains lie. Since I was a young priest I have followed Padre Pio from a distance. Now, to have seen where he lived, to have visited his cell, the refectory and the altar on which he said Mass, the confessional where he passed the greater part of the day, was for me a most touching experience. With the sincere hope, if this should correspond to the designs of providence, that the cause for beatification of Padre Pio may go happily forward, I thank you for the kindness shown to me on the occasion of my visit.[7]

Another well-known cardinal, who emerged in the eyes of the whole world for his contribution to the Second Vatican Council, particularly with reference to liturgical reform, voiced his deep appreciation of Padre Pio. This was Giacomo Cardinal Lercaro, Archbishop of Bologna, a stronghold of communism for many years and one of the most difficult episcopal sees in the whole of Italy. Cardinal Lercaro is also widely known for his works on mental prayer which have been translated into several languages. Speaking of Padre Pio he said:

> I remember my first meeting with him many years ago. I found him in the choir of the little church of Our Lady of Grace, in the place where he usually prayed. I was very glad, even though it meant that I had to wait some time before seeing him. Obviously I could not take him away from his colloquy with God. It seemed to me that this was exactly where he should be found, at prayer. His early morning Mass in the midst of the people (where he was almost rapt in ecstasy) and his silent prayer there in the deserted choir, these were in fact the roots of that supernatural strength which gave substance to his enlightened words, words that were gruff and harsh at times, but also persuasive and most comforting.[8]

The saintly Cardinal Ildephonse Schuster, predecessor of Cardinal Montini in the See of Milan and whose own cause has been introduced in Rome, had high words of esteem for Padre Pio, although there is no record of his having visited him. "It seems to me," wrote this holy prelate, "that Christian suffering is such a sublime charism, uniting us more fully with the Lord, that it is to be preferred to many other charisms such as ecstasies and the like. Padre Pio, in San Giovanni Rotondo, has suffered the agony of his wounds for over thirty years."[9]

The dynamic Archbishop of Naples, Corrado Cardinal Ursi, has visited San Giovanni Rotondo many times in recent years and is a fervent devotee of Padre Pio. When the magnificent Stations of the Cross, the work of top Italian sculptor Francesco Messina, were inaugurated in May 1971 on the pineclad slopes close to Padre Pio's tomb, Cardinal Ursi delivered a memorable address which was fully reported in the friary's official magazine for the cause of beatification. As befitted the occasion he spoke at length of Padre Pio's sufferings.

During his whole life Padre Pio lived the mystery of the Cross. He was a man who suffered as Christ suffered, who was crucified with Christ. He bore sufferings of every description, humiliations, misunderstandings and betrayal, cheerfully and calmly, obedient to God even unto death, as Jesus was. His sufferings were caused not merely by men, for the demons also loaded him with intense moral and physical suffering. From dawn to dusk, moreover, the moral disorders, sufferings and despair, the product of sin, converged on him from all parts of the world, carried there by the innumerable penitents who crowded around his confessional.

Padre Pio's life was one uninterrupted sacrifice. For many years he lived shut into his little religious community. There was no travelling, no preaching, there were no religious ceremonies except holy Mass, therefore no relief from the daily round, no consolations. The variety of ministries brings a certain relief. For him all was monotonous as he remained for interminable hours in the confessional, exposed to the demands of the crowds who sought him and who often acted with uncontrolled fanaticism, which hurt and grieved him as was sometimes quite evident. His preaching, his apostolate consisted in his silence filled with God and his immolation in the confessional. His silent powerful witness was like a slap in the face for so many who consider the apostolate to consist in activism, organisation, material means, technical equipment and so forth, while they underestimate the value of the interior life, of prayer, humility, obedience and sacrifice. Words, organisation and technical means are useful, it is true, but the essential thing is the witness which consists in possession and irradiation of the Spirit of God.[10]

During the International Eucharistic Congress held in Philadelphia in August 1976, Cardinal Ursi took part in the Padre Pio Programme at the Civic Centre, which was thronged for the occasion. His hearers were deeply impressed by the Cardinal's stirring words on the life and virtues and holiness of the stigmatised friar of Mount Gargano.

Another distinguished cardinal, Mgr Giuseppe Siri, Archbishop of Genoa, whose name is well-known outside his native Italy, has made several strong statements on the subject of Padre Pio's extraordinary life. When the Genoese "prayer groups" assembled in 1972, as they do each year, to commemorate the passing of the Servant of God, the Mass was celebrated by Cardinal Archbishop Siri who afterwards addressed them. He referred particularly to Padre Pio's letters which had appeared in Italian a short while previously. "I think that any one who wants to get to know Padre Pio, rather than reading a biography should read his letters," said the cardinal. He then went on to speak of the "mystery which synthetises the life and mission of this great man. In him was renewed the passion of Jesus Christ, insofar as this was possible in one who was not the Son of God. This is everything. Padre Pio of Pietrelcina is contained in this statement." In the course of his long address, the cardinal related a personal experience of his own. He told how he had been passing through a period of great perplexity with regard to a problem to which he could see no solution. "Then, one day," he said, "a telegram arrived from Padre Pio in which he urged me to take a certain course of action. I don't remember ever having spoken to any one about the matter and I have never discovered how this man could have known my state of indecision. But there was the telegram telling me what to do. I followed it to the letter and the whole matter was happily settled." Cardinal Siri's entire address on this occasion is most stirring and reveals his deep conviction with regard to Padre Pio's mission in the Church. "Our age needs people who offer suffering to God, who offer what his only-begotten Son endured. In my opinion Padre Pio is not the only one to suffer such suffering, but he is certainly the most noteworthy manifestation of this in our own century."[11]

Cardinal Siri never visited San Giovanni Rotondo during Padre Pio's lifetime, but he followed the events of his life with deep interest, culminating in complete conviction about the Capuchin's genuine holiness. Invited by the Capuchin friars to preach at the commemorative ceremonies in San Giovanni Rotondo in 1975, the cardinal accepted and spoke this time to a congregation from all parts of Italy and from some other countries. On that occasion he referred to Padre Pio as one of the beacons which down through history have given light to men. "Here today," he said, "we are honouring one of these beacons, one who continued in a marvellous way during life and – it would seem – continues in death the work of evangelisation."[12]

When important visitors, including many Church dignitaries, began to arrive at the little friary as early as 1920, the visitors' book came into being. Padre Pio was then only thirty-three years old, but his fame had spread far afield and his ministry already reached out to vast numbers. It would make monotonous reading if we were to list all the prelates who signed the book and left an enthusiastic message in its pages. It would also make tedious reading if the comments of a great number of Italian bishops naturally more numerous than those from further away, were to be quoted. Just a few examples will serve as an indication of what these high ecclesiastics thought of the stigmatised friar who received them with such deep respect and humility.

Mgr Gaetano Pollio, Archbishop of Salerno and formerly Archbishop of Kaifeng, one of the largest dioceses in China, came at the head of 1,400 pilgrims to Padre Pio's tomb in 1971. His homily during the Mass was a fervent exhortation to "firm faith, love of prayer, obedience to the Church, after the example of Padre Pio".[13] Mgr Achille Palmerini, Bishop of Isernia, Venafro and Trivento (an inland diocese about eighty miles north of Naples), in an address in September 1972 said, among other things:

> Padre Pio made suffering his daily food. This wonderful man whose life is in great part a mystery, this man who was not understood during his lifetime and by many is not understood now that he is dead, chose to suffer from early childhood. This man at the foot of the cross relived with burning love Christ's entire Passion and applied it first of all to himself, a poor sinner, as he called himself. The true saint, in fact, considers himself the greatest sinner in the world. Padre Pio recommended himself to the prayers of his confessors, his fellow-friars and his penitents, that the Lord might have mercy on him. But the sins by which he was weighed down were not his own; they were the sins of those who came to him, those sinners whom he recognised by a special light of the Holy Spirit; they were sins committed in all corners of the earth. Padre Pio took them all upon himself, just as Christ on the cross bore the sins of all mankind.[14]

The present Archbishop of Manfredonia, Mgr Valentino Vailati, under whose direction the preliminary diocesan cause was terminated and sent to Rome, is a frequent visitor to San Giovanni Rotondo, where he has preached with conviction on many solemn occasions in honour of Padre Pio. On 23 September 1972, commenting on the gospel of the day, the parable of the sower *(Lk 8:5-15),* Mgr Vailati said:

> Padre Pio is certainly one of those who "hearing God's word, held it fast in an honest and good heart" so that it grew and yielded a hundredfold. During his whole life Padre Pio opened his heart to the divine word, he savoured it, meditated deeply on it and gave it a vital place in his life, so that he was transformed by it even to the marrow of his bones. He was a Capuchin friar who first absorbed the wisdom of God and then communicated it to the countless numbers who had recourse to him.[15]

Mgr Andrea Cesarano, who governed the See of Manfredonia previously for a great many years, was equally convinced of the holiness of this friar who continued to attract more and more visitors to the diocese. Mgr Paolo Carta, at present Archbishop of Sassari (Sardinia) and formerly Bishop of

Foggia, has already been mentioned in these pages as a staunch supporter of the stigmatised Capuchin. He has returned to Padre Pio's tomb as guest preacher more than once during the special celebrations held each September to commemorate the stigmatisation of 1918 and Padre Pio's holy death fifty years later. The text of his four sermons in September 1976 has appeared in *The Voice of Padre Pio,* Vol. VII, Nos. 1-4, 1977, under the general title of "The Man of God" and the subtitles "Who Prays", "Who Suffers", "Who Absolves", and "Who Offers".

Great numbers of Council Fathers took advantage of the "free days" between their assemblies in St Peter's Basilica to travel to San Giovanni Rotondo. They came in a continual stream during the months when Vatican II was in session, prelates from all parts of the world, anxious to meet the holy Capuchin and recommend their intentions to his prayers. A vast collection of photographs of these distinguished visitors is kept in the records of the friary. Long before those memorable years of the Second Vatican Council, the visitors' book bore the signatures of many foreign bishops. A brief entry dated 2 July 1939 synthesises the sentiments of Mgr Alfredo Viola, Coadjutor Bishop of Salto, Uruguay: "I have passed two days of paradise here." At a much earlier date, 25 October 1921, we find the signature of Augusto Cardinal Silli: "With great spiritual benefit I visited Padre Pio in the friary of San Giovanni Rotondo." An even earlier entry is still more eloquent, signed by the Carmelite Bishop of Allahabad (India), Mgr Angelo Poli. Dated 2 July 1920, it runs: "Veni, vidi et victus sum. [I came, I saw and I am conquered.] I have no doubts. The hand of God is here."

Acts of fanaticism there certainly have been around the person of the holy Capuchin whom God favoured with such remarkable charisms in a little hill town of one of the poorest regions of Italy, just as superstition and fanaticism are frequently to be found wherever the supernatural enters the lives of men. But we can pass over all such puerile manifestations as unimportant when we consider, on the other hand, the innumerable expressions of esteem for Padre Pio voiced by popes, cardinals and other high dignitaries of the Church.

SEVENTEEN

His Holy Death

Dawn was breaking on 23 September 1968 when the tele-
phone rang loudly in the Bari office of the *Gazzetta del
Popolo,* a daily newspaper widely read in southern Italy.
There was just one employee on duty at that hour and he
hurriedly took up the phone. Over the wires came the voice
of the Chief of Police in Foggia: "Have you heard the news?
Padre Pio is dead." Like lightning that news travelled all over
Italy and to many places abroad. Within a few hours people
were flocking by every available means of transport to San
Giovanni Rotondo, by car, by train, by plane from further
away, by slower means from the entire rural region around
Mount Gargano. The scene was quite unparallelled as about
100,000 people converged on the little town on the slopes of
that barren mountain. A seemingly endless crowd moved
forward with difficulty up the hill during the entire four
days in which Padre Pio lay in his open coffin in that large
church, which had been completed less than a decade
earlier to accommodate the throngs who attended his Mass.
Then came the funeral rites and the procession three miles
long which accompanied the mortal remains of the beloved
Capuchin through the town. The event figured on the front
pages of many Italian newspapers and received great publicity
in many other countries.[1]

The end had come so suddenly that his devotees could
hardly believe it. When the friary bell began to toll its mournful notes they were already waiting as usual at the church
door, ready to assist at his early morning Mass. The stigmatised friar had been with them only a few hours earlier. It
was true that he had become very feeble in the preceding
months. His feet and legs were so painfully swollen that he
was frequently accompanied from his cell to the sacristy in
a wheelchair, and by a special dispensation he sat at the altar
to say Mass. The holy friar's heart ached with sadness, more-

over, because of the losses he had suffered during the previous year: the death of his beloved elder brother, Michele, at eighty-five, and of his faithful collaborator over so many years, the holy American tertiary, Miss Mary Pyle, laid to rest close to Padre Pio's parents in the local cemetery in April 1968.

The day preceding his death was a busy one for the aged friar. His "prayer groups," officially approved by the Holy See in July 1968, had assembled in large numbers in San Giovanni Rotondo on 22 September for their fourth international meeting. The church was far too small to contain them all when Padre Pio said Mass that morning at the usual hour, 5 a.m. A large platform had been erected in the square for their meetings. At 10.20, before the proceedings began, Padre Pio came to the window of the old church to greet his spiritual children and to bless them. He then blessed the first stone for the new stations of the cross. He was very feeble, but the friars and those around him had become accustomed to this. He was constantly assisted by another friar, but no particular attention was paid to his condition on that day which immediately preceded his death. He remained in his cell for most of the day and at noon was heard reciting the Our Father, slowly and deliberately, in a loud clear voice. In the afternoon he went to his usual place in the gallery above the altar and from there, as was his custom, he blessed the expectant crowd in the large new church below. Nobody suspected that this was his last blessing and the last glimpse they would have of him in this life. After dark the "prayer groups" assembled by torchlight in the field beneath his cell, expecting to see him at the window, but he did not appear.

The account of Padre Pio's last hours is best told in the words of Padre Pellegrino, the friar whose turn it was to assist him that night.

Shortly after 9 p.m., when Padre Mariano had retired and I had taken up duty in Cell No. 4, which was connected with Padre Pio's by intercom, he called me. I went along and found him already in bed, lying on his right side. He merely asked me to tell him the time by the alarm-clock which was there on his bedside table. His eyes were red and I wiped some tears from his face. Before midnight he called me again five or six times. Each time I went to his cell I found his eyes red with weeping, but it was what I may describe as gentle, peaceful weeping. About midnight he begged me like a little child to remain with him and from that moment onward he continually asked me to tell him the time. He looked at me imploringly and squeezed my hands. Then, as if he had already forgotten what I had told him about the time, he asked me: "Have you said Mass?" I I replied with a smile that it was too early for Mass, then he said: "Well, this morning will you say it for me?" I told him I said Mass every morning for his intentions.

Padre Pellegrino remarks that Padre Pio usually asked him to say Mass for his intentions, while this time he said "say it for me". His assistant began to be a little worried when Padre Pio, who had not slept at all, asked him to hear his confession. He was not his regular confessor but had sometimes obliged the aged friar. He continues his account: "After confession he said to me: 'My son, if the Lord calls me today, ask forgiveness from my confrères for all the trouble I have given and ask them and my spiritual children to say a prayer for my soul.'" Padre Pellegrino reassured him but had a slight presentiment of something unusual at this point. He asked him for a blessing for the friars, for his spiritual children and the patients in the hospital. Padre Pio replied: "Yes, yes, I bless them all. In fact, I ask the Superior to have the goodness to give this blessing on my behalf." All this was unusual but by no means alarming, for, as his companion remarked, Padre Pio was just the same as on any other night. He seemed quite normal and was not troubled by the usual distressing attacks of asthma. Moreover, he was quite calm and continued to pray. But a little later he asked his assistant to let him renew his act of religious profession. Padre Pellegrino recalls:

At about 1 a.m. he said to me: "Listen, son, I'm not able to breathe properly here in bed. Let me get up. I'll be able to breathe better there on the chair." He was accustomed to rising at one, two or three o'clock to prepare for Mass. Before sitting down in the armchair he used to walk up and down a little in the corridor. That night I observed to my great surprise that he walked easily and erect like a young man, so much so that it was not necessary to have him lean on my arm. When we got to the door of his cell he said: "Let's go out for a moment onto the verandah." I followed him there, with my hand under his arm. He himself switched on the light and when we came to the easy chair he sat down and looked around him as if searching for something. After about five minutes he asked to return to his cell. I tried to support his weight, but he said: "I'm not able", and, in fact, he had begun to sag heavily. "Don't worry, Padre", I said, and at once I got his wheelchair which was just a few feet away. I took him under the arm and eased him into the chair and he himself placed his feet on the footrest. When we reached his cell and I had settled him in his armchair, he pointed to the wheelchair and said: "Take that outside." When I returned to his cell immediately afterwards I noticed he had turned very pale, while his forehead was wet with cold perspiration.

I became alarmed when I saw that his lips were livid. He had begun to repeat without ceasing: "Jesus! Mary!" in a voice that was growing weaker at every moment. I moved towards the door to call one of the friars, but he stopped me and said: "Don't waken any one." I went out just the same and had begun to hurry down the corridor when he called me back. I returned, thinking he needed something, but when he said agàin: "Don't waken any one", I implored him: "Padre, let me go now." I ran out towards Padre Mariano's cell, but seeing the door of Brother Bill's cell open, I put on his light and shook him saying: "Padre Pio has had a bad turn." In a moment Brother Bill reached Padre Pio while I ran to telephone Dr Sala, his own physician. After about ten minutes the doctor arrived and, the moment he saw Padre Pio, began to prepare an injection. When it was ready, Brother Bill and myself tried to lift him but without success, so we eased him onto the bed. The doctor gave him the injection and then helped us to put him back in the armchair, but the usual reaction did not take place.

Meanwhile, summoned by Dr Sala, several others arrived: Mario Pennelli (Padre Pio's nephew), the head physician from the hospital (Dr Gusso), accompanied by the anaesthetist, Dr Scarale. I myself had called the Guardian, Padre Mariano, and some other members of the community. The doctors administered oxygen with cannula and mask and as he grew weaker they even tried artificial respiration, but there was no response. Then Padre Paolo of San Giovanni Rotondo anointed him while the other friars knelt around him in prayer. He was conscious of all that went on and he continued to repeat almost imperceptibly the same words: "Jesus! Mary!" His lips continued to form the words even when his voice was no longer audible. He was calm and composed and during the last few minutes seemed to be sleeping. We didn't notice his last breath and were only aware that he was gone when his head dropped gently to one side. It was about 2.30 a.m.[2]

Padre Pio's own physician, Dr Sala, who was with him to the end, has testified to the complete disappearance of the stigmata immediately after Padre Pio's death, leaving no sign whatsoever, a fact, the doctor concludes, which is "outside all typology of clinical action and of a character beyond the natural".[3] Commenting on Padre Pio's stigmata in 1971, Corrado Cardinal Ursi, Archbishop of Naples, said: "Padre Pio also gave us a sign of the resurrection . . . He was wounded in his flesh, like Christ, in order to destroy evil and suffering in the world of today, but immediately after his death the flesh which had been injured by the mysterious wounds was renewed . . . an indication of the certainty of final resurrection . . . and also to show forth the credentials of his special mission for the good of his fellowmen."[4]

Although Padre Pio's fame had spread abroad, perhaps nobody suspected the worldwide impact his life had made until those days immediately following his death. The foreign press took up the news and continued to publish articles concerning this extraordinary man. Radio programmes in Italy followed the course of events in San Giovanni Rotondo, while unexpected coverage was also given to Padre Pio on foreign programmes. The friars of his community listened with astonishment to these widespread reactions to the passing of their holy confrère and recorded many of those broadcasts, which are kept in the archives of the friary. Testimonies poured in from all parts. The authoritative Vatican organ, *L'Osservatore Romano,* carried a special article. "From all parts," it ran, "believers and the sceptical hastened to Padre Pio, drawn by the fame of his virtue. People spoke of special supernatural gifts and on this point the Church will pronounce in due course. We can only say that Padre Pio consoled and brought back to God innumerable souls; he reconciled men who were far from the faith and Christian life, sometimes enemies of religion." A well-

known Italian writer described him as "a friar bowled over by
his love for others". This same writer made an attempt to
estimate the numbers who had sought Padre Pio in San
Giovanni Rotondo. His estimate may well fall short of the
reality. "In fifty years," he wrote, "Padre Pio heard about
600,000 confessions. The pilgrims who went there numbered
about three million. Those who claim to have returned to the
faith because of his words amount to several thousands;
converts to Catholicism from other religions, several hundred."
A southern Italian daily headed an article with the words:
"He spoke for half a century to the heart of the world."
Another referred to him as "an example of silent dedication
to the priestly and monastic state, yet in the midst of the
world which proclaims the death of God". An atheist described
his own conversion in another newspaper: "I went to see him
when I had a thousand reasons for not believing in God.
With great delicacy, little by little, he led me back to the
faith and gave me the moral stability I lacked."[5]

There were touching scenes among the crowds who mourned
him during those days of his funeral rites. People told each
other of the extraordinary things he had accomplished in their
lives. A photographer who had often been indiscreet in his
attempts to photograph Padre Pio during life and had been
rebuffed by him many times, taking a photograph during
the funeral, said, "Now he'll never rebuke me any more!"
and then abandoned himself to bitter weeping there in the
public square.

As the funeral procession streamed through the town
there was an atmosphere of chilled bewilderment, a great
void in the hearts of the mourners. "It was as if the sun had
suddenly disappeared for ever", comments G. Contarino in
the article already quoted. The Franciscan order was represented by a large group of friars, students and aspirants who
surrounded the hearse. Along with the municipal authorities
of San Giovanni Rotondo were those from other towns,
notably Foggia and Pietrelcina. Professor Enrico Medi, the
atomic scientist who had been his friend and penitent for
many years, commented on the mysteries of the Rosary with
inspiring words which evoked the events and virtues and

extraordinary life of the deceased Capuchin. The mayor, at that time Dr Sala, paid a moving tribute to the illustrious citizen of San Giovanni Rotondo when the procession reached the centre of the town. Then the long mournful cortège wound its way uphill once more to the square in front of the church. Here solemn requiem Mass was con-celebrated by the Capuchin General, Father Clement of Wlissinger and twenty-four priests in the presence of two bishops.

The final scene of this moving drama was enacted in the crypt when the coffin containing the precious remains of the holy Capuchin was laid in the austere marble tomb where it is venerated today by innumerable pilgrims.

In October 1966, speaking to his niece, Pia Forgione Pennelli, Padre Pio had clearly foretold his own death. "In two years time," he said, "I won't be here, I'll be dead."[6] Precisely on 22 September 1968, the eve of his death, work was completed on the crypt where he was to be buried and Padre Clemente went down to bless the burial place. As far back as 1923, in those painful days when the order had come from the Capuchin Superiors for Padre Pio's transfer to another region, the Provincial had appealed to the mayor and the local police for help and protection in carrying out this order, in view of the threatening attitude of the local people. On that occasion Padre Pio himself, who was quite ready to obey the order received, wrote a farewell note to the mayor to assure him that he would always remember "these gener-ous people" in his prayers. Then he continued: "As a sign of my love for them, since I am unable to do anything more, I desire, if my superiors make no objection, that my bones may be laid in some quiet little corner of this place." The original Italian text of this message may be read today on a marble slab near his tomb in the crypt. That "quiet little corner" had been made ready to receive his holy remains less than twenty-four hours before his death!

EIGHTEEN

His Works Live On

The outstanding institution which perpetuates the memory of Padre Pio is his magnificent hospital in San Giovanni to which he himself gave the name Casa Sollievo della Sofferenza (Home for the Relief of Suffering). Travelling by the usual route from the fertile plain around Foggia, pilgrims to his tomb suddenly find themselves in a surprisingly barren region as the road climbs the steep slopes of Mount Gargano. Then suddenly, as they round a bend, this immense building comes into view, an altogether incongruous pile in such a setting.

The history of this hospital is a history of faith and immense trust in God's providence and of deep suffering on the part of Padre Pio and his courageous associates in the vast undertaking. When Padre Pio came to the friary on Mount Gargano towards the end of World War I, the most elementary health and hygiene services were lacking in this area, with dire consequences for the poverty-stricken population. When crowds began flocking to his friary, attracted by his extraordinary life and charisms, there were hundreds of sick and suffering among them who hoped to obtain relief through his intercession. Thus, during his first years on that barren mountainside the problem of pain and disease and lack of medical care was constantly before his eyes. Mainly through his efforts, a small hospital was opened in the town in 1925, but it could only accommodate a very small number of patients at any one time. The idea of building an adequate hospital for the whole area was born one January day in 1940 in Padre Pio's own cell, where he was discussing the situation with three close friends: Dr G. Sanguinetti, a physician from Florence, Dr M. Sanvico, a veterinary surgeon from Perugia and Dr C. Kiswarday, a chemist from the extreme north-eastern limb of Italy which now belongs to Yugoslavia.[1] All three men were to be his generous collaborators in the great enterprise which sprang from Padre Pio's immense compassion for the sick and suffering. A small committee was set up, but Italy's entry into the war put a stop to its activities for several years. As soon as the conflict ended, contributions began to arrive for the realisation of Padre Pio's project and in 1946 it became necessary to form a limited liability company, which was formally set up in Foggia. Spring 1947 witnessed the first stroke of the pick on the stony surface of the mountain close to the friary. A year later the foundation stone of the hospital was laid. Although many people were contributing by this time, the cost of the enterprise by far exceeded the financial resources. Then, suddenly, things began to happen.

Barbara Ward in London, engaged to be married to Lord Jackson, a non-Catholic, heard about Padre Pio and came to ask his prayers for the conversion of her future husband. Rather disappointingly, Padre Pio merely told her that if God so willed her fiancé would become a Catholic. "But when?" she asked. "If God so wills, now," was Padre Pio's reply. To the lady's great surprise, on her return to London she found that her future husband had already been baptised a Catholic. While in San Giovanni Rotondo she heard about the hospital and the immense sum of money it required. Her fiancé became deeply interested in the project and through the medium of these two influential people a grant amounting to about £200,000, a very large amount of money at that time, was contributed by the United Nations Relief Agency towards the building of Padre Pio's hospital.[2] There is a curious aftermath to Lady Jackson's interest in the hospital. In the artistic chapel on the second floor, the image of Our Lady depicted in the stained-glass window above the altar bears a startling resemblance to Lady Barbara Jackson! A typically Italian expression of gratitude to the renowned economist.

In July 1954, to Padre Pio's great satisfaction, the "relief of suffering" began, when the hospital's day-dispensaries opened. The hospital proper, by no means as large as it is today, was officially opened in May 1956. This unique institution aimed at twofold assistance of the sick: medical treatment of the highest quality and moral and spiritual care of the patient at the same time. With this end in view, personnel were carefully chosen from the beginning and soon a nurses' training school was added.

Padre Pio gave much thought to the future of this institution which God's providence had made possible. The limited company set up in 1946, a temporary solution for the building and running of the hospital, was to last ten years. Just as this period was ending the official opening took place, on 5 May 1956, Feast of St Pius V and Padre Pio's own feast-day. By that time, as a result of deep thought and much prayer on the part of Padre Pio and his close collaborators, a solution had emerged. With the consent of the Holy See and of the Capuchin General, responsibility for the hospital was to be taken over by a special branch of the Third Order of St Francis to be set up for the purpose in San Giovanni Rotondo. A number of well-wishers and benefactors had been approached, mostly people who had been guided for years in the spiritual life by Padre Pio, including doctors, lawyers and other professional men. Fifty of these asked to be admitted to this branch of the Third Order of which the Director was Padre Pio himself and for which special rules had been drawn up with the approval of the competent authorities. In December 1955 the Capuchin General travelled to San Giovanni Rotondo to perform the ceremony of admission, during which each member received the scapular and cord of St Francis from his hands. These close associates of the holy stigmatist included one English speaker, Mr John McCaffery, who had been living in Italy for a number of years. Of Scottish birth and Irish ancestry, Mr McCaffery now lives in Co. Donegal. He has recently written an interesting book entitled *The Friar of San Giovanni: Tales of Padre Pio.*[3]

* * * * *

As the years passed and the face of Italian society underwent many changes, Padre Pio, weighed down by the sufferings and fatigue of his almost eighty years, pondered still on the future of his hospital, desirous above all that the genuine spirit of the institution should be preserved. The hospital's finances, at his own request, were already in the hands of the Holy See, through the Institute for Religious Works, more commonly known as the Vatican Bank. Now, on 11 May 1964, the founder of the Casa Sollievo penned his last will and testament by which he donated the hospital to the Holy See. Shortly after his death Vatican officials took over the management.

Since the opening of the hospital in 1956 additional wings have been built. A large community of nursing sisters was installed before long. Medical congresses take place from time to time in premises specially equipped for the purpose. In 1978 Padre Pio's hospital had a capacity of 900 beds while the indoor staff of sisters and nurses numbered 150. The hospital owns two large farms in the area which provide wine, olive oil, grain, meat and other products for its daily needs. A prelate from the Vatican lives on the premises as president of the council responsible for the efficient running of the institution. Three Capuchins are in residence to care for the spiritual needs of the sick. A large church is incorporated in the building, while there is a chapel on another floor, and there are frequent Masses on Sundays with at least three on weekdays. The benefactors of this charitable institution so dear to Padre Pio's heart have continued to increase in number and a fund supported by contributions from many countries covers the expenses of patients who are unable to meet their own bills.

A magazine entitled *La Casa,* published fortnightly in Italian and less frequently in other principal European languages, informs a large circle of friends of all that goes on at this centre of charitable activity founded by Padre Pio. This is also the central office for his prayer groups which received the approbation of the Holy See in 1968 shortly before he died. There are now, ten years later, more than 1,000 of these groups, of which 700 are in Italy and the remainder distributed throughout other European countries, Asia, Africa, North and South America, and Australia. Each group is directed by a priest.

Before he died Padre Pio predicted that a number of

charitable works would spring up on Mount Gargano and that San Giovanni Rotondo would become a veritable city of prayer and good works. His great heart went out to embrace all the physical and spiritual needs of suffering mankind and his earnest desires are gradually being fulfilled.

Less than a mile downhill from the friary a new institution opened its doors in January 1971, inaugurated by the Archbishop of Manfredonia in the presence of the local authorities and numerous benefactors. This is the rehabilitation centre for spastic children. Spastics in Italy in the early nineteen-seventies numbered more than 300,000, most of them in the less developed regions of the south where Padre Pio spent his whole life. Recent progress in the treatment of spastic children has made it possible to improve their condition through a process of muscular re-education. In the modern spastic centre in San Giovanni Rotondo, about 100 children receive daily care and treatment. The majority come from families in San Giovanni itself, but buses go out each morning to collect little sufferers from other small towns on Mount Gargano, so that they also may avail of the special therapy and general loving care which is lavished on all in this institution. A small community of Franciscan nuns is in charge, with a staff of twenty-seven, including teachers, social workers, therapists and domestic staff. A pleasant family atmosphere has been created in this centre to which spastic children from tiny tots to eighteen-year-olds arrive each morning in time for a substantial breakfast.[4] Two further spastic centres were opened in the early seventies, the first in Manfredonia, about fifteen miles away, and the second in Termoli, a coastal town to the north of Mount Gargano. All three centres are under the direct control of the Capuchin friary in San Giovanni Rotondo.

The spiritual needs of many people are also catered for in San Giovanni Rotondo. Groups of priests assemble there frequently to make their annual retreat close to Padre Pio's tomb. Quite recently a building which was formerly a hotel, not far from the friary, was modernised to enable large groups of lay people with their priests to spend a few prayerful days there. A small community of nuns took over the management of this house in 1976. In a smaller house not far away a little group of dedicated women cater for retreat groups on a smaller scale. There is talk of setting up an organisation to cater for the aged, especially those who have remained alone in the world. These activities were already present to Padre Pio's mind as he viewed the various problems of suffering humanity and yearned to be of service to all classes of people. Slowly but surely his desires are finding tangible expression.

Less tangible, but none the less real, is the work of works which continues to grow and flourish there in the remote little town in which he passed most of his life: the conversion of men's hearts. People of all classes and from the most varied environments come in increasing numbers to his tomb, many of them nowadays from Ireland, England and the United States. Some arrive there for the first time, propelled by many different motives, sometimes without any clear idea as to why they have come. None of them, or certainly very few, leave San Giovanni Rotondo without experiencing a deep awakening to spiritual values, sometimes a complete renewal of faith and hope, sometimes a lightning conversion. This was the case continually with those who encountered the holy stigmatist during his lifetime, and this is still happening today. His visible works, the hospital and similar activities, live on to perpetuate his memory, but his invisible action in the souls of men has not ceased with his passing from this world. He is reputed to have said: "After my death I will do more. My real mission will then begin." To judge by the scene around his tomb today, his words would appear to have been prophetic.

Notes

PREFACE

1. Padre Pio da Pietrelcina, *Epistolario*, Vol. I, 2nd ed., Capuchin Friary, San Giovanni Rotondo (Foggia), 1973. Two further volumes have appeared in Italian: Vol. II, 1975, containing Padre Pio's correspondence with a holy woman named Raffaelina Cerase; Vol. III, 1977, containing his correspondence with various lay persons. A fourth volume, not yet in print, will contain his correspondence with priests and religious. The English edition of Vol. I is now available at the Capuchin Friary in San Giovanni Rotondo, entitled: Padre Pio of Pietrelcina, *Letters*, Vol. I, *Correspondence with his Spiritual Directors*.
2. A quarterly magazine in English, *The Voice of Padre Pio*, is also published by the friary.

PROLOGUE

1. Letter to Nina Campanile, Nov. 1922, in *Epistolario*, Vol. III, p. 1006.
2. Don Nello Castello, *Gesù Crocifisso in Padre Pio*, Casa Mariana, Frigento, Italy, 1976, p. 14.
3. *Ibid.*, p. 15.

ONE   EARLY YEARS

1. Adelia Mary Pyle, born of wealthy parents in New York in 1888. As a close collaborator of Maria Montessori, foundress of the Montessori, system of children's education, she travelled widely. She was twenty-five when she became a Catholic. In 1923 she visited San Giovanni Rotondo and met Padre Pio. Shortly afterwards she settled near his friary, where she died and was buried in 1968.
2. Fernando da Riese, *Padre Pio da Pietrelcina*, Capuchin Generalate, Rome, 1975, p. 44.

3. Our Lady has been honoured in the whole region around Pietrelcina under this title for many centuries, ever since the liberation of the city of Benevento from the Greeks through her intercession in the seventh century.
4. Alessandro da Ripabottoni, *Padre Pio da Pietrelcina*, Capuchin Friary, Foggia, 1974, pp. 40ff.
5. *Ibid.*, pp. 43-4.
6. *Ibid.*, pp. 48-50.
7. *Ibid.*, pp. 50-52.
8. *Ibid.*, p. 55.

TWO   VOCATION

1. Alessandro da Ripabottoni, *op. cit.*, p. 57.
2. *Ibid.*, pp. 59-62.
3. Padre Pio of Pietrelcina, *Letters*, Vol. I, Appendix: Autobiographical Notes.
4. Padre Pio of Pietrelcina, *Epistolario*, Vol. III, pp. 1005ff.

THREE   PREPARATION FOR A MISSION

1. Alessandro da Ripa, *op. cit.*, p. 108.
2. *Voce di Padre Pio*, Oct. 1971, p. 20.

FIVE   MYSTICAL ASCENT

1. *Letters*, Vol. I, *cit.*
2. "The Man of God who Prays," in *The Voice of Padre Pio*, Vol. VII, 1977, No. 2, p. 15.
3. *Letters*, Vol. I, *cit.*, Introduction: Concomitant mystical phenomena.
4. *Ibid.*
5. *Ibid.*
6. *Ibid.*
7. *Ibid.*
8. *Ibid.*

SIX   HIS SPIRITUAL DIRECTOR

1. *Complete Works of Saint Teresa,* Sheed and Ward, London, 1975, Vol. II, p. 23.
2. Padre Pio of Pietrelcina, *Letters,* Vol. I, *cit.*
3. *Self-Abandonment to Divine Providence,* Collins, London and Glasgow, 1974, p. 120.
4. Riccardo Fabiano, "Padre Benedetto Nardella" in *Voce di Padre Pio,* July-August 1972, p. 22.

SEVEN   A MODEL FRIAR

1. One of the physicians sent by the Superior General of the Capuchins in 1919 to examine Padre Pio. Dr Festa's report on his examination of the wounds is amply quoted in Chapter 15.
2. *Voce di Padre Pio,* December 1974, p. 7.
3. Padre Giovanni da Baggio, *Padre Pio visto dall'interno,* Capuchin Provincial Records, Florence, 1970.
4. *Ibid.,* p. 8.
5. *Ibid.,* p. 11.
6. *Ibid.,* p. 23.
7. *Ibid.,* pp. 28-29.
8. *Ibid.,* p. 48.

EIGHT   A UNIQUE CONFESSOR

1. "The Man of God who Absolves," in *The Voice of Padre Pio,* Vol. VII, 1977, No. 3, p. 14.
2. *Ibid.,* p. 15.
3. See Chapter I, Note. 1.
4. See Preface, Note 1.
5. Padre Pio da Pietrelcina, *Epistolario,* Vol. II, Capuchin Friary, San Giovanni Rotondo, 1975, English edition not yet available.
6. Don Nello Castello, *op. cit.,* pp. 62-64.
7. *Ibid.,* pp. 68ff.
8. For the full text of Pope Paul's words on this occasion, see Chapter 16, 2nd paragraph.
9. Don Nello Castello, *op. cit.,* pp. 75-76.
10. Corrado Cardinal Ursi, Archbishop of Naples, in *Voce di Padre Pio,* July-August 1971, p. 3.

NINE   A SEVERE DIRECTOR

1. *Summi Pontificatus,* 20 Oct. 1939.
2. Condensed from "Gleanings" in *The Voice of Padre Pio,* Vol. VI, 1976, No. 4, pp. 10ff.
3. Condensed from "Gleanings" in *The Voice of Padre Pio,* Vol. VII, 1977, No. 3, pp. 6-7.
4. Padre Giovanni of Baggio, *op. cit.,* p. 24.
5. *Ibid.,* p. 31.
6. *Ibid.,* pp. 33-34.
7. *Ibid.,* pp. 61-63.

TEN   HIS CHARISMATIC GIFTS

1. Don Nello Castello, *op. cit.,* pp. 103-4.
2. From *Voce di Padre Pio,* July-August 1973.
3. From various Italian Franciscan publications.
4. *Voce di Padre Pio,* June 1971, p. 14.
5. Don Nello Castello, *op. cit.,* p. 105.
6. *Ibid.,* pp. 93-4.
7. *Voce di Padre Pio,* February 1972, pp. 18-19.
8. Don Nello Castello, *op. cit.,* pp. 82-3.
9. *Ibid.,* pp. 84-5.
10. Padre Pio of Pietrelcina, *Letters,* Vol. I, Nos. 82, 95, 96.

ELEVEN   PADRE PIO'S MASS

1. Fernando da Riese, *op. cit.,* p. 462.
2. Address delivered in San Giovanni Rotondo on 10 August 1975 and published in *The Voice of Padre Pio,* 1976, Vol. VI, No. 4, p. 13.
3. Mgr Antonio D'Erchia, Bishop of Monopoli (Bari), in *Voce di Padre Pio* July-August 1973, p. 12.
4. Lino da Prata and Alessandro da Ripabottoni, *Beata te, Pietrelcina,* San Giovanni Rotondo, 1976, pp. 44-45.
5. "The Man of God who Offers," in *The Voice of Padre Pio,* Vol. VII, 1977, No. 4, p. 15.
6. Padre Giovanni of Baggio, *op. cit.,* p. 17.
7. See Chapter 17, "His Holy Death".

TWELVE   THE DEVIL'S ASSAULTS

1. From an article in *Voce di Padre Pio,* Jan. 1972, p. 8.
2. *L'Osservatore Romano,* English edition, 23 Nov. 1972. p. 3.
3. See Note 1.
4. Padre Agostino of S. M. in Lamis, *Diario,* 2nd ed., S. Giovanni Rotondo, 1975, p. 56.
5. *Ibid.,* pp. 59-60.
6. Padre Alberto in *Voce di Padre Pio,* Oct. 1972, p. 16.
7. *Complete Works of St Teresa, cit.,* Vol. I, p. 205.
8. Pope Paul VI, Address to General Audience, *cit.*

THIRTEEN   HIS LOVE FOR THE CHURCH

1. Padre Bernardino of Siena, OFM Cap., in *Acts of First Meeting on the Spirituality of Padre Pio,* San Giovanni Rotondo, 1975, pp. 131-153.
2. *Dogmatic Constitution on the Church,* No. 21.
3. See *Voce di Padre Pio,* July-August 1972.
4. *Misteri di scienze e luci di fede,* no longer in print.
5. *Diario, cit.,* pp. 78-79.
6. See Chapter VII: *A Model Friar.*
7. "Padre Pellegrino Says 'No'", in *The Voice of Padre Pio,* Vol. VI, 1976, No. 2, pp. 11-12.
8. Letter written on 12 September 1968.

FOURTEEN   OUR LADY IN HIS LIFE

1. The historical information contained in this chapter is taken from *Beata te, Pietrelcina, cit.*
2. *Marialis Cultus,* Nos. 44-47.
3. *Ibid.,* No. 41.
4. This chapter has been adapted from an article by the same author entitled "Our Blessed Lady and Padre Pio" which appeared in *The Voice of Padre Pio,* Vol. VII, 1977, No. 2.

FIFTEEN   WITNESSES TO THE STIGMATA

1. "The Stigmata of Padre Pio," in *Acts* of the above meeting, pp. 101-129.
2. *Voce di Padre Pio,* September 1973, p. 7.
3. *Voce di Padre Pio,* June 1974, p. 5.
4. *Acts, cit.,* p. 120.
5. *Voce di Padre Pio,* December 1974, p. 9; January 1975, p. 7 and February 1975, p. 7.
6. Vol. VI, 1976, No. 4, p. 12.
7. *Ibid.*

SIXTEEN   THE VOICE OF THE HIERARCHY

1. *Voce di Padre Pio,* March 1971, p. 3.
2. *Ibid.,* September 1972, p. 15.
3. Fernando da Riese, *op. cit.,* pp. 458-463.
4. *Ibid.,* p. 460.
5. *Ibid.,* pp. 460-461.
6. Vatican letter to Padre Pio, No. 7886, 27 January 1959.
7. *Voce di Padre Pio,* March 1976, p. 12.
8. *Ibid.,* February 1977, cover.
9. Writings of Cardinal Schuster under examination in the Cause for his Beatification.
10. *Voce di Padre Pio,* July-August 1971.
11. *Ibid.,* March 1973, pp. 14ff.
12. *The Voice of Padre Pio,* Vol. VI, 1976, No. 3, p. 9.
13. *Voce di Padre Pio,* July-August 1971.
14. *Ibid.,* March 1973, p. 12.
15. *Ibid.,* November 1972, p. 16.

SEVENTEEN   HIS HOLY DEATH

1. *Voce di Padre Pio,* September 1972, p. 15.
2. *Ibid.,* September 1973, p. 5; cf. also *L'Amico de Terziario,* Capuchin Friary, Foggia, special number, November 1968, p. 50.
3. *The Voice of Padre Pio,* Vol. VI, 1976, No. 4, p. 12. For Dr Sala's full statement see Chapter XV: *Witnesses to the Stigmata.*
4. *Voce di Padre Pio,* July-August 1971.

5. G. Contarino, in *Voce di Padre Pio,* November 1973, pp. 7-8.
6. Fernando da Riese, *op. cit.,* p. 440.

EIGHTEEN HIS WORKS LIVE ON

1. Alessandro da Ripabottoni, *cit.,* p. 372.
2. *Ibid.,* pp. 380-381.
3. Darton, Longman and Todd, London, 1978.
4. For a full account of the work of this Rehabilitation Centre, see *The Voice of Padre Pio,* Vol. VII, 1977, No. 2, pp. 10-12.